Step Back

NORMAN DRUMMOND

First published in Great Britain in 2015 by
Hodder & Stoughton
An Hachette UK company

This paperback edition first published in 2016

1

Copyright © Norman Drummond, 2015
Illustrations copyright © Rob Pepper

ISBN 978 1 473 61480 2
eBook ISBN 978 1 473 61479 6

Typeset in Sabon by Hewer Text UK Ltd, Edinburgh

Printed and bound in the UK by Clays Ltd, St Ives plc

Hodder & Stoughton policy is to use papers that are natural, renewable and recyclable products and made from wood grown in sustainable forests. The logging and manufacturing processes are expected to conform to the environmental regulations of the country of origin.

Hodder & Stoughton Ltd
Carmelite House
50 Victoria Embankment
London EC4Y 0DZ

For
Katie and Amy and Logan
Beau and Gracie
our wonderful grandchildren,
who all give their Grandad and Nana
personal lessons in how and when to Step Back

Contents

Part 2:

The Many Ways of Stepping Back

Acknowledgements

Special thanks are due to Ian Metcalfe, my Director of Publishing at Hodder, who first came up with the idea of *Step Back ... finding the way forward in life* and who has offered such helpful and sterling advice. I am also indebted to my experienced and talented Editor, Caro Handley, and my indefatigable Assistant, Wilma Shalliday, all of whom along with me have been under the aegis and experienced guidance of my Agent, Kay McCauley of the Pimlico Agency in New York, to whom I will be ever grateful.

Every effort throughout has been made to source and gain permission to use material. My apologies if there are errors, which the Publishers will endeavour to correct at the earliest opportunity.

I wish to pay tribute to Peter Armitage of Ardoch, our gracious benefactor of Columba 1400 Loch Lomond which, along with our original Columba 1400 Centre in Staffin on the Isle of Skye, provides regular opportunities of *stepping back* every day of the year.

Peter has been typically encouraging in always asking *"what are you writing?"* and *"when's the next book?"* – as indeed have been the tireless contributions over the years of the talented and devoted Columba 1400 Team of whom the now over 8,000 Graduates here in the United Kingdom and across the world are their best possible adverts and commendations.

One of the real joys of being a Father and a Grandfather is to see the next generation coming through and leaving you as it were in their wake. In that regard my eldest son Andrew, who is now responsible for Drummond International, has been a constant source of wisdom and encouragement not only in the writing of *Step Back* but also in the faithful practice of such in his increasingly busy life.

During the writing of *Step Back* a most unexpected pleasure for us as a family has been to meet with my late Father's best school friend, Michael Paton, now in his 95th year and still going strong. My Father, Edwin Drummond, died when I was only 19 and so Michael's presence and advice has meant a great deal to me and in no small measure has encouraged me to 'Step Back' ... in order to go forward in life.

Foreword

Norman Drummond's book details his busy life in a number of fields where he has made a real difference. His experience, amongst his many other achievements, as Headmaster of a major Scottish school and as a Minister of the Church of Scotland was an ideal background to found and Chair Columba 1400, a hugely enterprising social initiative and charity which has helped young disadvantaged people in Scotland face the future with confidence.

As Patron of Columba 1400, I have seen his work at first hand and this book passes on the lessons the Reverend Drummond has learned throughout his life – not least, the importance of reflecting, as this book does for our benefit.

Anne

All of humanity's problems
stem from man's inability
to sit quietly in a room alone.

Blaise Pascal

Introduction

As founder and chairman of Columba 1400, the social enterprise and charity that is so close to my heart, I oversee an organisation that helps young people to find their unique voice and purpose and to face the future with confidence. As chairman of Drummond International I work with business leaders as an executive coach and mentor, conduct leadership forums and retreats, and speak at a range of events from graduation ceremonies to international business conferences.

I am also a minister of the Church of Scotland, so I am often asked to conduct weddings, funerals and other services alongside various pastoral responsibilities.

Then there is my family – the source of enormous joy and love: my wife Elizabeth, my five children and my five grandchildren. When all of us get together, as we often do, it's quite a gathering – noisy, full of laughter and great fun.

I enjoy everything that I do, but I couldn't do it if I

didn't take time, regularly, to recharge, review and renew.

I believe that many of us are shrinking through lack of the space simply to 'be'. We're running hard yet going nowhere, and we're denying ourselves the joy and the opportunity for growth and understanding that comes with stepping back; that is, stepping out of the race for a little while and taking the time to be peaceful and alone.

That is why I am writing this book.

Like most of us, I wear a lot of hats and combine many roles. I could not possibly balance and maintain all the different aspects of my life and work if I did not regularly 'step back'. I follow a demanding schedule, travelling, speaking and coaching all over the world. I wouldn't be able to keep up the pace or be there for others in the way that I wish to if I didn't pause regularly for reflection.

Stepping back is not simply the means by which I top up my own energy and enthusiasm for life. It is at the core of all I do: as a mentor, as a coach, as a minister, and as a father and grandfather, I encourage others to 'step back' from the hurried detail of their own lives in order to gain insight, perspective and inner calm. I'm not a therapist or a lifestyle guru, but I have spent a lifetime observing and reflecting on human experience, and I've learned a great deal, from my own experience and from that of others, about what makes people tick and what they need in order to feel happier, stronger and more connected to one another.

This journey started for me when I decided not to go into law, which I had studied at university, but to work instead in the ganglands of Glasgow with a charismatic minister called Bill Christman. There I saw such potential going to waste among the young people, either through the way in which the system was run or through their lack of self-esteem, that I promised myself I would get back there one day to help those same youngsters.

Over twenty years later, in 1997, I kept that promise when I began the work of Columba 1400, a social enterprise and charity named after the Celtic prince who became St Columba – and founded 1,400 years after his death. We opened our first purpose-built centre on the Isle of Skye in 2000, followed ten years later by a second centre in Loch Lomond. At these centres we welcome young people from 'tough realities', along with their teachers and mentors, to bespoke Leadership Academies, during which we encourage them to step back from what they know, in order to find their way forward in life. Columba 1400 now has over eight thousand graduates across the United Kingdom and overseas, with suitably tailored operations in Australia and South Africa. These young people are now leading lives of meaning and purpose.

What we teach them is that life is not about figures or facts or bottom lines of measurement. It's about interactions, knowing yourself better, working hard to enable

3

others to achieve, truly knowing who you are and aspiring to what you might become. When this becomes the focus of what you are doing, life is more selfless and purposeful and therefore joyous.

In this book I want to pass on all that I have learned in my own life about the value of stepping back – as well as sharing the valuable, enlightening and sometimes unusual stories of others who have stepped back in order to go forward.

It may seem deceptively simple, but I believe that stepping back is the key to breaking through barriers, self-imposed or otherwise; to finding answers, whether these are spiritual, emotional or practical; and to living a life that is richer, fuller and more worthwhile.

Learning to step back will restore balance and rhythm to your life, and will allow you to first recognise within yourself, and then to develop, the three qualities that are vital to anything worthwhile in life:

Integrity
Courage
Openheartedness

With these three qualities embedded in the way we think and feel, we can and will discover our true selves and realise our authentic purpose in life. Stepping back will allow you to listen – really listen – to yourself and to others. It will enable you to assess – or perhaps reassess – people and situations with understanding and compassion. And it will bring you clarity of thought and strength of belief so you can pursue your life goals with harmony, meaning and purpose.

Prologue
Why Step Back

Modern life is relentlessly busy. The calls of work life and home life are many and varied, and if there is any spare moment then there are emails to check, messages to answer, or social media to update. It seems impossible to get off the treadmill.

The answers to life's most pressing and important questions can, I believe, only be found in solitude and in slowing down. If we don't give ourselves time for this kind of reflection, we forget what is meaningful and valuable.

We hurtle along, leading a frantic life, working longer hours, doing more and more – for our children, and perhaps for parents too – and seldom getting enough deep, nourishing sleep, fresh air or healthy food. We dig deeper and deeper with fewer and fewer resources until life feels out of control and we become exhausted, or ill, or both. It is increasingly common now for people to find themselves in a post-viral or deeply fatigued state.

If you're feeling overstretched and overloaded, with

never a minute to spare and no time to think or stop, then it's very hard to keep perspective on your life and what's going on around you, or to open the door to change. Many of us fill every waking minute with something to do. We flip from phone to iPad to laptop, work long hours, plan purchases and holidays – and then we wonder why we feel exhausted and over-wrought, or as though something is missing in our lives. We end up with what I think of as a 'mind like mince' – so mixed up we are unable to focus success-fully on any single thing.

Being busy can get in the way of your creativity and passion. It can also be a way to avoid facing a problem or taking on something new and different. 'I'd love to but I'm just so busy' can easily become a mantra.

A life led in this way is saying no to maintaining the rhythm and balance necessary for fulfilment and no to making a difference in the world around you. It is a limited life which cannot offer satisfaction. Yet many of us continue to be puzzled by this.

Are you 'spiralling'? A life spiralling out of control, at the mercy of external pressures, has no space for joy or wisdom. It is perfectly normal for busy people to feel overwhelmed by the demands of life now and then, but to feel that way is a warning sign and to ignore it is to rush headlong towards unhappiness and ill health.

If life feels like this for you, then the time has come for change. And the simplest, most effective change you can make is to 'step back'. Stepping back shouldn't be an optional extra in our lives, it should be a priority, to refuel us and to help us cope with all the other demands we face.

Some of the most famous military commanders in history, among them Napoleon Bonaparte, Admiral Horatio Nelson and General Dwight Eisenhower, all recognised this and insisted on a period of relief and rest for troops in action, so that they were able to regenerate in body and spirit and with that renew their courage and determination.

Most of us can recognise the benefit of slowing down and taking time out for reflection, but in many cases we have reached the stage where we have stored up so much inner exhaustion that when we do stop it feels as if we might never get started again. It can feel like trying to jump off a speeding bus – if we do ever get off, we'll never manage to get on again. If you feel that way, though, it's time to ask yourself: 'Is this really the bus I want to be on?'

Run your life; don't let your life run you, or let it be run by others

Slowing down and allowing yourself periods of deeper reflection, away from the round of daily duties and responsibilities, is quite simply life-changing. It can be of immeasurable benefit.

By doing this you provide yourself with an opportunity to reframe your mindset, and to realign and reorder the tasks you have set yourself. You are giving yourself the gift of time, to notice, to enjoy and to take pleasure in things that normally pass you by – the beauty of nature, the taste of good food, the joy of music.

Slowing down, by stepping back and reassessing your life, gives you time to focus on people and on priorities. You may find it unnerving to let go of familiar supports such as your phone, iPad or laptop, but none of those help you to feel fully present: they are distractions. Your inner soul needs complete attention if you are to listen to it. Those things get in the way of stepping back. To know ourselves fully present through a period of slowing down rekindles our confidence and courage and allows us to get things into perspective.

While many people in busy firms and offices may tell you that there's no time for slowing down, the fact is that there is *always* time for what matters. On the one hand, stepping back and slowing down often leads to periods of greater output, creativity and productivity. On the other, time out for reflection and renewal is always time well spent. It leaves us wiser, healthier and mentally stronger – better able to give our all.

So when should we choose to 'step back'?

I believe we all need to take time for ourselves regularly, no matter what our circumstances. But there are certain times when it becomes the *one thing* that will restore our peace of mind, hope and belief in ourselves.

If any of the following hits home, you know it's time to step back:

- You are uncertain, overwhelmed or tired.
- You are facing a decision, confronting a difficulty, unsure about the way to go about a task.
- You are sad, lonely, heartbroken or hurt.
- You are feeling frustrated, misunderstood and helpless.
- You are anxious, worried, concerned.
- You feel you are living life at the wrong pace.
- You lack confidence.
- You feel trapped.
- You are looking for a direction in life that has meaning and purpose.
- You are so embedded in the routine of your life that you feel it is losing its meaning.
- You feel that you have no real control over your life.

Stepping back is deceptively simple and powerfully effective, yet most of us *never* do it. Once it becomes a regular practice, however, the benefits are immense and unlimited. They may surprise you, liberate you and delight you. It's time to make a change.

There is more to life than increasing its speed.

Mahatma Gandhi, lawyer,
leader of the Indian National Congress
and advocate of non-violent protest

Part 1
The Rich Rewards of Stepping Back

While the initial effort to 'step back' may feel challenging, the benefits and advantages are profound. Indeed, in my opinion the benefits are so profound that once stepping back is a part of your life, you will wonder how you managed without it.

There are many ways in which stepping back can help you reorient and refocus in your life. Here are what I believe to be the twelve most powerful and effective benefits of taking time to step back.

What is the difference between an obstacle and an opportunity? Our attitude toward it. Every opportunity has a difficulty, and every difficulty has an opportunity.

Sidlow Baxter, pastor and theologian

I love the man that can smile in trouble, that can gather strength from distress and grow brave by reflection.

Thomas Paine, author,
political theorist and revolutionary

1

Choose Your Attitude

I've never been a big believer in training manuals. While of course I know there's a role for training, it isn't someone's training that makes me decide whether I want to work with them or not, it's their attitude.

When I come across someone whose attitude to a job is 'I can do this, and if there's something I can't do, I'll learn', then I know I've found a person who will be good to have around.

The one thing you can choose in life is your attitude. American author and pastor, Charles Swindoll made this observation:

The longer I live, the more I realise the impact of attitude on life. Attitude is more important than the past, than education, than money or circumstances, than failures or successes, than what other people think, say or do. It's more important than appearance, giftedness or skill.

We cannot change our past, or the fact that particular people will act in a certain way. Nor can we change the inevitable. The one thing we can do is to play as well as we can on the one string we have, and that is our attitude.

The remarkable and wonderful thing is that you do have a choice, every single day, regarding the attitude you will embrace for that day. And the choice you make will affect everyone you come across and all that happens during your day.

You can make a conscious effort to set the tone for the day that lies ahead of you, and you can do that best by spending just a few minutes quietly stepping back as the day gets going. You can't choose all of the events in your day, but you can choose how you set out to deal with them.

I say a short prayer every morning, usually seated in a quiet place, often with an inspiring passage or verse in front of me. If I'm pressed for time I might be saying that prayer as I get out of the shower or clean my teeth. I ask blessings for those who are in need, and I dedicate my day to being of use and service. That small moment of prayer guides my day. I'm not a believer in the 'you pray – you get' school of thought. I don't think that prayer is about asking favours, expecting everything to go my way. I would rather think of it as 'you pray – you give', because to me there's no greater joy than feeling, at the end of the day, that I might have made a positive contribution or helped someone make a difference in their life.

It's good to review things, to look at whether you might have done something differently for a better result, to ask yourself searching questions. But if you constantly berate yourself or allow yourself to feel that you can't get anything right, then you will grind to a halt, and that doesn't help anyone.

The Ultimate Qualification: NQGE

If I'm coaching someone I often make a little note in the margin of my notes as I'm listening to them relating their life story or experience. Pretty often, one of those notes might say 'NQGE'. And what does NQGE stand for? Never Quite Good Enough.

NQGE has no place in a scientific or medical text book, it's not a qualification recognised by any exam board, but it most definitely has a defining role in everyday life for lots of people today. So many of us have been brought up by those who thought they were doing the right thing or the best thing by pushing us on the one hand and minimising praise on the other. The result is often that we grow up berating ourselves for not doing better, no matter what we achieve. Even the best results end up being qualified with a 'Could have done better'.

When I come across a case of NQGE, I encourage the sufferer to step back for a moment and reflect on where the message came from, and then to begin giving themselves a new message: MTGE, or More Than Good Enough.

I recently met a man called Chris who suffered from a serious case of NQGE. He was the first in his family to go to university and went on to achieve his doctorate before becoming a senior university lecturer. He was proud of his achievement, yet he suffered from a serious case of NQGE, which stemmed from the fact that he never heard his father recognise or compliment him throughout all those years of hard work. It was only after his father's funeral, when his mother turned to him and said, 'You were the light of your father's life, you know, he was so proud of you,' that he learned how his father had really felt.

It turned out that his father had never stopped telling his friends all about him – but he had never expressed those feelings to his son. Chris burst into tears. He needed a period of stepping back to reflect upon and reframe this before he could go forward in life reassured by the knowledge that he had been good enough after all.

Chris was lucky – he discovered that his father really had been proud of him, and that helped him enormously in re-evaluating his view of himself. But while positive messages from others are wonderful when we are lucky enough to receive them, we can't count on them: the real work of reframing, of moving from Not Quite Good Enough to More Than Good Enough, has to happen within us.

One of the biggest obstacles to seeing yourself as good enough is the drive for perfection. Many of us feel that we should somehow be perfect, but since not one of us *is* perfect, to strive for such an extreme is a thankless task at which we are all bound to fail. It is better instead to strive for focus and self-discipline, which are possible, and to cultivate kindness, good humour, tolerance and compassion. If these wonderful qualities are what you nurture and develop in yourself each day, then you will be up to dealing with anything that comes your way, no matter how challenging.

At a packed communion service in the ancient abbey on the Scottish Island of Iona, that cradle of Christianity, the minister asked the congregation to put their hands up if they felt perfect or were leading lives of perfection. No one moved. He then asked the congregation to put their hands up if they felt broken, betrayed, resentful and in need of renewal and strength – at which a forest of hands went up.

No doubt all those who raised their hands at Iona that day were relieved to see how many others did so too. We all feel tired and resentful. We all know we are a long way from perfect. But if you can learn to feel good enough, you will be able to let go of so much frustration, pain and blame.

It is quite possible to put aside resentment and other negative feelings. If something hurts or upsets you, refuse to let it affect all your actions and thoughts. By stepping back and seeing that it is a small issue in the wholeness of your life, you can usefully compartmentalise it and lessen its hold on you.

Part of my personal journey has meant learning to accept that 'perfect' isn't achievable – that most of the time, in this imperfect world, it is more than OK to settle for 'good enough', with the occasional 'great' or even 'fantastic'. That's been frustrating sometimes. I want to give any project, large or small, my absolute best, and it's humbling to realise that even your best can't manage everything or fix every problem.

Perfectionists tend to want to be in control and to do everything themselves. But there is a joy in letting go of trying to get things perfect, and a large part of that lies in realising how much others have to contribute, and that a joint endeavour is infinitely preferable to going it alone. When you accept that perfect isn't a realistic goal, it's much easier to share, to delegate or even to step aside when someone else can do a job better than you can.

Singer Leonard Cohen, who seamlessly combines a Jewish background with being an ordained Buddhist monk, often expresses his lifelong support for the oppressed and the downtrodden in his songs, along with a gentle and humorous acceptance that none of us will ever be perfect.

'Anthem', written in 1992, sums up perfectly the value of not getting what you want, of getting it wrong and of imperfection. The chorus goes like this:

> *Ring the bells that still can ring*
> *Forget your perfect offering*
> *There is a crack in everything*
> *That's how the light gets in.*

He expresses so beautifully this truth that I have so often felt – that not only is this platonic ideal of perfection impossible, it isn't even desirable. There is a joy and beauty that comes through imperfection. I often refer to Cohen's lyrics, because he expresses so clearly and wisely the need to resist self-aggrandisement and triumphal egotism. His music has a resonance for people who are struggling with anything in their lives, as most of us are at some point. And he reminds us, gently but insistently, that perfection, far from being perfect, is an illusion that can only disappoint us, whereas only the acceptance of imperfection will bring us as close to peace and harmony as it is possible to get.

The plain truth is that perfectionism isn't particularly easy to be around, but a positive attitude in a person who feels comfortable and at ease with themselves is deeply attractive; we are drawn to it like moths to a flame. How much more we learn about life and love and laughter when the perfect doesn't work out!

There is one prayer that, over the years, has had the

most resonance for me. It was first given to me by Ronnie Selby Wright, a great friend and mentor of mine, who was the Radio Padre during the dark days of the Second World War:

> *Do not pray for easy lives.*
> *Pray to be stronger men and women.*
> *Do not pray for tasks equal to your powers.*
> *Pray for powers equal to your tasks.*
> *Then the doing of your work and the living of*
>   *your life shall be no miracle.*
> *But you shall be a miracle.*
> *Every day you will wonder at the richness of life*
> *Which has come to you through the Grace of*
>   *God.*

The message here is wonderfully empowering. There's not much point in praying for things to be simple and straightforward, because a fair percentage of the time they just aren't. But if you pray to be up to coping with whatever comes your way, you will discover inner strength, courage and confidence.

So 'step back' each day, and set your attitude for that day. Choose to bring smiles to the faces of the people you encounter, choose to be patient, understanding, kind and supportive, to yourself and to those around you.

You see things that are and say why? I dream of things that might be and say, why not?

George Bernard Shaw, Irish playwright,
co-founder of the London School of Economics

I have learned that success is to be measured not so much by the position that one has reached in life as by the obstacles which one has had to overcome whilst trying to succeed.

Booker T. Washington, leading voice of former
African-American slaves

2

Find Your Path

Are you, perhaps unknowingly, preventing yourself from pursuing what you truly want to do? When it seems that our path is blocked, or we feel we're heading in the wrong direction, we almost always blame this either on others, or on our circumstances.

The truth is that it is down to us. If you feel blocked – in your work, in a relationship, in what you are able to manage or achieve in life – then you need to examine fully your own part in creating, or at least tolerating, this block on your potential. There may be apparently 'good' things in your life of which you need to ask: does it serve a useful purpose? For instance, know when to leave a committee to free up time for other things, or if Twitter is going nowhere for you, don't tweet – and if you're working most weekends, it may be time to stop.

Sometimes what is familiar just feels comfortable and is hard to let go of, even if it is holding you back.

It takes courage to go beyond what is known, what feels comfortable, and to push back the boundaries we place around ourselves. We know our home, job, family, activities; we repeat our routines and patterns. We are all of us creatures of habit; we like to know what is happening and where things are going. So to make a real, significant change, to ask for more, to try something new, to take a big decision or to set out on a new venture can feel terrifying. But if we never do this, our lives will be poorer for it, because we will never know how it might have turned out. Whereas if we take a chance and throw a large pebble into the still waters of our lives, we might just discover that the impossible is possible after all.

Making space in your life to step away from its daily demands and to give yourself time to reflect, to be peaceful and to enjoy beauty and stillness – perhaps in something as simple as the raindrops on a leaf or the shape of an acorn – is a wonderful way to start the process of shifting whatever may be blocking your progress. By stepping back, you can see the things that are filling your time unnecessarily and you can decide where and when you need to say no in order to allow new ideas and directions to take root.

In his book *The Power of Silence: The Riches that Lie Within*, former journalist and BBC economics correspondent Graham Turner describes learning to spend short periods in silence and the enlightening discovery of the wise voice inside him that he had not been aware of before. 'I never suspected just how rich, important and fulfilling silence can be, how universal its usefulness.' He said he knew, just in those short times, that there were several things he needed to do, to put right and to change, in order to move forward.

Many companies nowadays expect employees to keep a work phone, laptop or tablet on and with them at all times. And even if it's not a requirement, employees feel the pressure to be always available. Recently one company in the United States decided to allow their employees one evening off a week. During that time they were not expected to have their phones or other devices on and were free to have the time to themselves. To the company's surprise, productivity increased. The employees felt liberated, knowing that on one evening a week they could make an arrangement and know they would keep to it, or could just choose to relax. That little bit of space reaped great dividends. And so it is with all of us. If we give ourselves a little space, we will find ourselves recharged and able to function far better.

It is a wonderful truth that by seemingly doing less, you can achieve more, whereas by remaining perpetually busy you block your own creative energy and wind up less effective even at the things you are most committed to. In the creative space of stepping back, allow yourself to dream of what you really want to do. Is it taking a step forward on your existing path, or a whole new direction? Be open to new ideas, to seeing things differently and appreciating different perspectives.

If your plans are to become more than just plans, of course, then you need to overcome the hurdles of speaking up and making changes. Everyone has a capacity to fight for what they know is important, but like a muscle that weakens with inactivity, if you are not used to being determined and motivated, it will feel strange at first. However, if you back away from the challenge to go out and make your dreams and goals happen, then your life will be poorer. Look deep inside to find the most determined and motivated part of yourself. If you rise to the occasion you will have the joy and exhilaration of realising that the impossible can become possible.

There are essential practical steps. Break your goal down into realisable targets. Everything is easier in stages, and having a working plan to guide you will help too. That said, don't aim too low – stretch yourself and aim for the highest possible achievement with each next step. If you think you can do one thing, then perhaps you can do even more. Be bold, believe and, most of all, be brave.

Then there is timing. Success or failure can come down to this. Is the moment right for what you have chosen to do? Good timing is a vital part of creating a life which is balanced and fulfilled, so reflect on your timing before you act.

There are two aspects to timing – first, allowing ourselves enough time, time to be sure, and time to be fully prepared; and second, judging when the time is right to take action and be successful.

Giving ourselves enough time means pausing in what may be the headlong rush of life, to slow down, take stock and measure the pace of our lives.

Take the time to 'chill and still'.

It is only when you are prepared to chill out that you can be still enough to listen to your own soul. Unless we do this we cannot function well, keep a clear perspective and make good decisions.

When we give ourselves enough time, we can be more effective in choosing the timing of major events in life. How can we know when the time is right to begin a project, change direction, face up to a boss or a parent or a child, or to make a change in our lives? When are the circumstances right? Getting the timing right often requires patience. Sometimes, however, we hesitate through fear, rather than patience. Fear can paralyse us, so make sure you're not hesitating for too long, numbing yourself into inaction through anxiety about the consequences. Better to be brave and act, even if later you decide that the timing could have been better. A door is never closed without another being opened – but we must be willing to walk through it.

To choose your moment as wisely as possible, ask yourself these questions:

- Do you know what it is that you want to do, change or achieve?
- Do you feel ready?
- Are the circumstances favourable?
- Have you mapped out the first few steps?
- Have you got support?
- Does your heart tell you that the moment is now?

The last question is the most important. If you feel, instinctively, that the time has come to make your move, then trust that feeling and act. Not through unexamined impulse but out of a deep, gut-level knowledge. That combination of certainty, excitement and anticipation, allied to a calm inner resolve, is marvellous and from it can come extraordinary results.

To determine your own path in life, refuse to be dictated to by others as to what you are going to do, which way to go, or who you are. Ask yourself the important questions and find your own answers. By all means consult people you trust, listen to advice, say your prayers. But don't let go of your capacity for self-determination.

The animals were all gathered in the forest talking among themselves. 'We hear there's a new animal coming among us,' some said. 'And he's got a list of who will die, and some of us are on the list.'

The new animal, a bear, duly arrived and the other animals regarded him with caution and concern. 'Does he really have a list? Which of us is on it?' they muttered to one another.

The lion stepped forward. 'I am the strongest of the beasts, so I will go and see him and find out,' he volunteered.

The lion went to the bear and said, 'I hear you have a list of all the animals that are going to die. Am I on the list?'

'Yes, you are on the list,' the bear replied.

The lion, depressed and downhearted, slunk away. And soon afterwards he died.

'I'll go next,' said the fox. 'I'm cunning, perhaps I can outwit him.'

He went to the bear. 'Am I on your list?' he asked.

'Yes,' replied the bear. 'You are on the list.'

The fox was so shocked he ran away as fast as he could. And soon afterwards he died.

The other animals looked at one another, fearful

and anxious. 'We'd better find out if we are on the list,' they said.

One by one they went to the bear, only to be told that they were on the list. And one by one they died.

Finally it came to the turn of the tortoise. He was slow, so he had not yet made it to the bear. But eventually he arrived and asked, 'Am I on the list?'

'Yes,' said the bear.

'OK, you can take me off the list,' said the tortoise. And he walked away and lived happily for a long, long time.

I like this story because it is so startlingly simple. If you don't like what is happening, don't go along with it. Choose to get off the list and find your own path.

It is meaningless work, not overwork, that wears you down.

John Bunyan (1628–88),
author of *Pilgrim's Progress*

If a problem is fixable, if a situation is such that you can do something about it, then there is no need to worry. If a problem is not fixable, then there is no help in worrying. There is no benefit in worry whatsoever.

His Holiness the Dalai Lama XIV

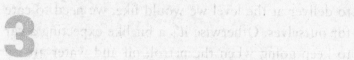

3

Care For Yourself

To wake up feeling well, fit, able and energetic is a gift – one that we all too often take for granted. It is often only when we become ill that we realise the most valuable thing we have is our health.

Do you care about your own health and well-being? Or do you push yourself too hard, sleep too little, put off exercising, eat too much fast food and allow stress to keep you tense and tired? If you don't care for yourself it can leave you exhausted, and exhaustion drains us and leads to hopelessness. We need to listen to our bodies more with each decade that passes, and to treat ourselves with care and respect.

In my work I frequently come across people who are overtired and constantly worried by minor ailments. Rather than address this they push on, ignoring the messages from their bodies and, as a consequence, potentially heading towards major health scares.

Many of us lead busy and demanding lives. We ask a lot of ourselves, mentally and physically. But in order to deliver at the level we would like, we need to care for ourselves. Otherwise it's a bit like expecting a car to keep going when the petrol, oil and water are all running out.

While there is no doubt that we need to eat properly, exercise regularly and get enough rest, an additional vital part of self-care is finding a way to practise releasing tensions and negative emotions, and at the same time to nourish and tend to the mind and spirit, which will in turn nourish the body.

The degree to which the external affects the internal, and vice versa, is now well known. Your mind affects your body just as much as what is going on in your body affects your mind. For example, doctors now believe that bitterness generates chemicals that affect our vital organs. These chemicals increase our heart rate, raise our blood pressure, disrupt digestion, tense our muscles, dump cholesterol into our bloodstream and reduce our ability to think clearly. Every time we mentally go over those bad feelings we deliver more corrosive chemicals to our body, leading to depression and ill health.

In a similar way, becoming rigid and tense on a regular basis actually tightens our internal organs to the point that it can restrict blood flow and hence hamper their smooth and efficient function. When you feel so tight that you can't easily take a full breath, it affects your whole body. Just as muscles can be strained, so too can our internal organs and our brains.

What all this means is that science is now confirming what the Scriptures have said over centuries: that forgiveness, of yourself and of others, is of deep significance. As it says in Proverbs 17:22, 'A cheerful heart is good medicine, but a crushed spirit dries up the bones.'

Some time ago a woman came to see me, feeling that something was blocking her way forward in life. Although she looked well groomed and had an outwardly successful life, she felt run-down and had little appetite. When we talked it soon emerged that she was constantly anxious and that she often compared herself to others and felt very critical and jealous. All of this was derailing her life and affecting her relationships with her colleagues, her husband and her children.

She agreed to come on a retreat to the island of Iona where, during two peaceful and reflective days, she peeled back the layers of her constant demand for perfection, from herself and others, to reveal a deeply held desire to live up to the very high expectations of her father. She chose to forgive herself for being less than perfect, and to accept that the only real perfection in life is found through accepting our imperfections.

Since leaving the retreat she has gone on to live a much happier and more peaceful life. Her health has improved greatly and she is less demanding of herself and of her family. She has become who she was meant to be, a person of great thoughtfulness, kindness and inner calm.

We are creatures of habit, and our habits form us. So to change what we are doing, if it is not in our best interest, we must change our habits – and that takes effort. Whether you are taking up exercise, making the decision to leave the office earlier, eating more healthily or beginning regular meditation, it will take you between two weeks and three months to fully establish a new habit. After that, though, you will actually miss your new behaviour if you don't keep it up.

In my own life I have recently discovered the joy and power of yoga. I visit a delightful teacher who, with gentle encouragement and great skill, has allowed me to discover more physical flexibility and the importance of breathing deeply so that it energises your entire being. The word 'inspire', after all, means, literally, to breathe. Most of us do not breathe deeply; our breath is shallow and short. To discover the remarkable effects of long, deep breaths – longer in than out – as in the yoga tradition is extraordinarily health-giving.

There are many other disciplines which encourage us to slow down and which are beneficial to good health, among them meditation or mindfulness and tai chi, originally a Chinese martial art, which involves deep breathing and slow, gentle movement.

Disciplines such as yoga and tai chi are not competitive and not about achievement. They are intended to enhance spiritual and physical good health.

Never underestimate the power of self-care. Not long ago I received a phone call from a woman I had never met. She told me that she had recently discovered a cache of letters to her husband from a woman he was clearly in love with. She had confronted him and he admitted his affair and left the family home.

Days later the woman had to take the children on a family holiday. It was pre-booked and rather than cancel and disappoint her children, she chose to take them on her own. As they set off she felt so low that she was contemplating ending her life. How was she to go on after being so betrayed by the man she loved?

At the airport she picked up a copy of my book *The Spirit of Success*, and on the journey she began to read it. When she rang she told me, 'It was the section on self-care that touched me most deeply. Your words reminded me that I have a lot to live for, and that I matter. By the time I came back from the holiday I no longer felt suicidal, I had decided to look after and appreciate myself, so that I could be there for my children.'

That story touched me deeply. The advice I had given in the book was very straightforward, most of it practical and simple. What the woman's words reinforced was how easily we can forget that we matter, that we are worth caring for and worth nourishing – whether that nourishment is a healthy meal, a new hairdo or a little time out.

We push ourselves so hard that we can forget to stop pushing. And we get tangled up in the small stuff. Someone once told me that you can tell a lot about a person by the way he or she handles these three things:

- a rainy day
- lost luggage
- entangled Christmas tree lights

Which of us hasn't got wound up over one of these, or something equally minor?

So many of us feel guilty about taking time out. Yet to do this, by stepping back, is to reinforce self-care in a powerful way. There's a lovely quote by American economist J. K. Galbraith in which he says, 'Total physical and mental inertia are highly agreeable, much more so than we allow ourselves to imagine. A beach not only permits such inertia but enforces it, thus neatly eliminating all problems of guilt. It is now the only place in our overactive world that does.'

If you haven't got a handy beach, as lovely as that would be, I do think it's entirely possible to find 'inertia' at home, if you are willing to put the demands of life aside for a short period every now and then.

We would all like to live with less stress, but without

working at it, it can't be done. It's all about those new habits.

Here are what I believe to be the seven most important habits we need to cultivate to live a healthier, less stressful life:

1. Eat well – lots of fruit, vegetables and healthy grains.
2. Exercise at least three times a week for thirty minutes, a wonderful antidote to stress.
3. Make room in your life for fun and relaxation.
4. Get eight hours of sleep when possible.
5. Maintain your sense of humour. Laugh often.
6. Forgive others; grudges are too heavy to carry.
7. Take time each day to be quiet and listen – to step back.

I heard a lovely story recently about a man who had lived a hectically busy life – until he was forced to wear a plaster cast on his leg for a year. He spoke of having a 'forced retreat' which had helped him to find a balance between action and reflection. He began a diary and started to meditate – and the impact of this enforced slowing down, coupled with reflection, was extraordinary. He said that he felt calm in a way that he had forgotten was possible. He found order and peace returning to his life and he felt better able to concentrate on family and friendships. Through all this his work did not suffer. He felt focused and creative and, while working fewer hours, was more productive.

What better encouragement could there be for all of us to slow down and step back?

To enjoy good health, to bring true happiness to one's family, to bring peace to all, one must first discipline and control one's own mind. If a man can control his mind he can find the way to Enlightenment and all wisdom and virtue will naturally come to him.

The Buddha

Start doing what is necessary; then do what is possible; and suddenly you are doing the impossible.

St Francis of Assisi, friar and preacher

4

Grow In Wisdom

Wisdom is the capacity to recognise what is of value in life. We need to understand the interconnectedness of all people and things, which means that any action, however small, will reverberate through a thousand other people and things around us. The wise listen, observe, attempt to understand and do not judge, and when they act they do so with care and insight. The wise also persevere, keep a clear perspective and know that sometimes all one can do is to put one foot in front of the other and keep going. They carry their knowledge lightly and are filled with humour and compassion.

In the western world we live in a society that judges knowledge to be of primary excellence and that values knowledge far more than wisdom. We admire people who know a great deal, who have endless facts at their fingertips and who can reel them off in a clever, sharp and witty way. But in the East, while knowledge is respected, the search for wisdom is considered more significant.

I believe we all have within us a well of innate wisdom – but too often we don't know it. Stepping back is a wonderful way to discover this innate wisdom, and with it greater clarity of vision and a powerful sense of what really holds value in life.

Wisdom also provides the route to inner strength and to knowing how to support yourself, physically and mentally, so that you can continue along your path in life, however tough that might be. Of course, knowledge is a wonderful thing, and we all need it. In our exam-based culture, we encourage our children to know facts if they are to succeed. But without wisdom, knowledge is a two-dimensional thing. It is not knowledge that will lead you to fulfilment, connectedness and joy, but wisdom.

We have seen some truly wise men and women in the modern world. I think first of Nelson Mandela, former president of South Africa; of Mother Teresa, founder of the Missionaries of Charity in Calcutta; and of Mahatma Gandhi, leader of the Indian National Congress, all now sadly departed. Each of these was filled with compassion for others and with humour, kindness and humility. They never threw their weight around or showed off their vast knowledge – quite the opposite, they claimed not to have any great knowledge. Yet they achieved extraordinary things, changing many lives and influencing many more in their pursuit of peace. Each of them knew suffering, frustration and pain, and yet never ever gave up on their goals and dreams.

In exactly the same way today, His Holiness the Dalai Lama, spiritual leader of Tibet, a wonderfully gentle and humorous man, exudes kindness and compassion, while never ceasing to pursue his quest for Tibet's freedom from Chinese rule. It is impossible to spend even the shortest time in his presence without feeling uplifted.

One of the qualities these four extraordinary people have in common is the ability to sustain hope in the face of great suffering and loss. With tenacity and strength of spirit they have managed always to see the bigger picture, and to pursue their aims in the context of the good of all. No matter what is happening in our lives, we too can cultivate hope and, with it, find a positive and effective way forward. In stepping back you can begin to find quietness and feel an inner, deeper power or presence that is your spiritual connection with hope. Whatever tough times you have come through, however painful or difficult, challenging or demanding life has been, with it will come a sense that this is not the beginning of the end, but rather the end of the beginning as your inner voice begins to affirm 'Yes' as opposed to 'No', 'Why not?' as opposed to 'How can I?'

By taking time to listen to the true workings of the human heart, one can begin to review the past, appreciate the present and look forward with courage and confidence to the future. With wisdom, then, comes the ability to restore the balance and rhythm of our lives. These two go hand in hand: though they are not the same, it is impossible to have one without the other, and they are the foundation stones of everything else.

Balance is about making room for the things that matter and not letting any one thing outweigh all the others. A balanced life has room for rest as well as work, for fun as well as seriousness, and for thought as well as action. With balance you can keep your feet on the ground while aiming for the stars. As Nelson Mandela once said, 'A good head and a good heart are always a formidable combination.' This captivating phrase encapsulates the essence of balance: kindness with wisdom, intellect with love, thoughtful concern with generosity.

Rhythm is what allows us to balance the different elements of life – to give each our all as we are doing it, but then to move on to the next thing wholeheartedly. Rhythm is good for the body, good for the heart and good for the soul; it is what enables us to achieve mightily in each area without getting burned out along the way. It is essential if you want to achieve anything worthwhile and long-lasting in your life and if you lose it, even for a short while, it needs to be rediscovered.

All of us have known times when our minds and bodies and souls have lacked rhythm and become out of balance. It is not a comfortable feeling when you are out of sorts in this way, when your shape is just wrong

48

somehow – particularly at a time when you want or need to be at your best. Inner dissonance leads to unease and thus can often open us up to dis-ease and illness.

In this fast-moving world countless men and women push themselves and their bodies well beyond rhythmic tolerances. 'Just one more call/visit/trip' leads to 'just a few more hours' at the workplace or in the office, an imbalance in your life and a toll on your health.

To maintain rhythm, we need frameworks and we need boundaries. Rhythm is far more than simply routine; it includes self-care and awareness, but routine is the essence, and this requires self-discipline. For instance, when you're under pressure, it's all too easy to let go of 'non-essential' aspects of life, like exercise. But if you know that you function better and sleep easier with regular exercise in your life, then you can determine that it is an essential, a necessity as important in your daily and weekly rhythm as the other essential elements that help you to maintain an overall balance.

Nelson Mandela attributed much of his success and achievement to the rhythm of his life. He was always well disciplined, even as a young man, and aimed to be the earliest, best prepared and best turned out for whatever might lie ahead in his day. Much of this he attributed to his early background in his village, where he was the son of a chief. And later, when he was imprisoned on Robben Island, he grasped victory from the embers by keeping a rhythm in his life that sustained him through the years. After his release, even as president of South Africa, he never failed to make his own bed before taking an early morning walk or period of exercise.

As you 'step back', take time to think about the essential components of your life – how will you keep balanced and in rhythm those things which are integral to your happiness and well-being?

It's important to look hard at your life and make sure that in addition to work you sleep enough, take time off, laugh often and spend time with the people you love and whose love means so much to you. Let me add that I believe it is also important to have in your life a third aspect of balance, what I often think of as the third leg of the stool: doing something for others. Just as a stool won't balance on two legs, our lives won't balance without the third dimension of *service*.

It's an old-fashioned word, but to me it is the key to spiritual fulfilment and joy.

Doing something for others is not about self-deprivation. It's about making a difference, contributing, caring and giving. Just as it's vital to look after yourself with care and love, because without that nurturing and nourishment you will run dry, it is also vital to offer support and love to others.

At Columba 1400 we have what we call our core values, and they are the basis of all that we stand for and the code we aim to follow and to share with everyone who comes to us. Around these core values we base the residential element of our six-day Leadership Academy, and with each day themed on one core value, we set out to create the conditions for profound individual change, through the discovery of each person's potential. While to some, looking on at our centre on Skye from the outside, it may appear to be just another outdoor centre, situated as it is in the middle of the mountains and lochs of this beautiful island, its real purpose is to go inward. The landscape is there to refresh, to be a backdrop to self-discovery and to give a sense of inner renewal through its beauty. But the real work for all those coming to Columba 1400 is to consider their internal state of being.

The Core Values of Columba 1400

Awareness

Self-awareness is the starting point in recognising your own beliefs and values. When you are willing to turn the spotlight inward and to look at all aspects of yourself, you demonstrate courage and discover what is truly important to you. Through self-awareness and the awareness and understanding of the people around you, you can begin to discover your leadership potential and the true potential of others.

Focus

Once you focus on what matters to you, energy and ideas and motivation will follow. Through focus you can begin to see what you wish to move away from, what is important to you and what you wish to achieve.

Creativity

Through creativity, cycles and patterns in your life can be changed. When you are fully aware and focused, the need for thoughtful action becomes apparent. Through this action we reach deep inside for the inner creativity which enables each and every one of us to be special and to make a difference.

Integrity

A deeply rigorous and strong sense of integrity is essential as you travel the road of self-awareness and of contribution. Integrity means being reliable and trustworthy and remaining true to your potential. Without it no code of values will stand up to the scrutiny of challenge, conflict or changing circumstances.

Perseverance

Perseverance means remaining strong and resilient when faced with complications, challenges and resistance. Nothing worthwhile is achieved without a deep, inner core of perseverance. Failure can often be the bedrock of success, and it is perseverance that keeps us going and allows strength of character and integrity to shine through.

Service

All the other core values lead to this one, the most important of all. The aware, focused, creative person of integrity and perseverance will find themselves led to the service of others. Service means sharing resources selflessly and effectively, believing that you can have a positive impact on your community and using your strengths and experience to take meaningful action and contribute to the greater good. In the service of others is the pathway to freedom, for in self-forgetfulness, self-fulfilment can be discovered and rediscovered time and time again.

We begin with these core values because we believe they are fundamental to building a sense of worth, to growing in confidence and to discovering potential. But at the same time we encourage each person, as part of their deepening self-knowledge, to identify and reflect upon their own core values.

In the search for wisdom, working out your own personal core values is paramount. During our Leadership

Academies we walk across the hills of Skye to a wonderful rocky outcrop called The Old Man of Storr, or perhaps to The Table on the magnificent Quiraing. The climbs are steep in parts, but far from impossible, and as we go we encourage participants to think about and focus on their personal core values. They start out with a list of perhaps twenty values they feel are important. At each resting place as they go up the hillside, they are asked to narrow their list down, so that by the time they reach the top, they have identified their six most important and most deeply held values.

Try this for yourself as a truly transformative stepping back exercise. Go for a walk – up a hill if you happen to be near one – and think about the qualities you most respect and admire and would like to embody. Narrow your list down to perhaps twelve qualities or values. Think about these for a while, then narrow that list down to six. This may not be easy, but it is better to focus on the few you think are most important. That way you will be better able to draw on them when you need them and to remember them in a crisis. These are your personal core values, the code by which you intend to live, your toolkit for facing any situation life throws at you and the basis of your sense of self-worth and purpose in life.

*The diamond cannot be polished without friction,
nor the man perfected without trials.*

Chinese proverb

*If you say you can or you can't, you are right either
way.*

Henry Ford, founder of the Ford Motor Company

5

Let Go Of Negativity

Negativity doesn't always come from others, of course. We all have our own inner negativities – doubts, fears and concerns. We can become negative without even realising it, and despite our loved ones pointing this out to us repeatedly, we can fail to acknowledge it. Unless we 'step back', reflect and review our lives, we can end up being more rigid than we would like to be and so allow a negative attitude to proliferate, sometimes unloading that unthinkingly into the lives of others, often without realising we are doing so.

The longer we live, the more we will experience of the ups and downs of life. Each and every one of us at some stage or other will have suffered pain or difficulty, betrayal and loss. When these things happen we can be in danger of spiralling into negative thinking, of feeling overwhelmed and believing that nothing will ever be the same again. We can drag ourselves down and affect all those around us who love us and are trying to help. We can become bitter and resentful, with all the damage that brings. Nelson Mandela said, 'Resentment is like drinking poison and hoping it will kill your enemies.' I'd put it this way: if you hold onto resentment, you're ruining two lives.

Why not let go of bitterness and resentment, right now, today?

To let go of such things is a profoundly spiritual act. As most of us know, it isn't easy to let go of hurt, grievance, bitterness, resentment and anger. To learn to let go is in truth a lifelong process. When you are able to put 'self' or 'ego' to one side, it becomes so much easier. Once you are not driven by ego, you can let go of defensiveness and with it the need to justify, hit back or take revenge.

All of us, without exception, experience things we need to let go of – there may be things in the past, or hurts and slights we experience, an attachment to someone who is not reciprocating, or pain and grief and bitterness.

Eric Lomax, whose book *The Railway Man* was made into a film, was a British army officer who, in the Second World War, was captured and tortured by the Japanese. He experienced depths of pain and hurt and depravity which we can scarcely begin to imagine. He suffered torture and despair, yet having let go of his past and taken the brave and courageous step to be reunited with his captor and to forgive, he was able to say, 'Sometimes the hating has to stop.'

When we begin to 'step back' and let go of our past hurts and fears, our sense of disappointment and failure, there comes the slow realisation that in many cases, no one is truly to blame. Misunderstanding one another's motives and actions is very easy, and many of our inner feelings of inadequacy are the marks of our earlier years, of feeling let down and disappointed in ourselves and others, of being made to feel small or inadequate, of never feeling accepted or good enough – to the extent that it becomes easier, almost more comfortable, to live in our inadequate past rather than to embrace a brave new future.

When you sell a house, it feels great to get rid of stuff you've accumulated. You wonder why you lived so long with it weighing you down. It's the same with mental and emotional clutter. The writer and business consultant Jon Gordon says,

> We fill our minds with thoughts that hold us back, habits that limit us, distractions that derail us, negative people who drain us, fear that paralyses us. We spend so much time and energy on things that don't matter that we fail to focus on what does matter. We fill up with so many things that generate negative energy, there is no room for positive energy in our lives.

Each of us has a long list of clutter, things we need to leave behind: here are a few that come up a lot, but I'm sure we all have our own collection.

- Believing that we are alone
- Trying to please everybody
- Feeling insecure
- Putting ourselves down
- Needing everybody to like us
- Jumping to negative conclusions before we know the facts

- Thinking we are always right
- Recalling all the times we messed up
- Wanting to know how it all turns out
- Needing to have all the answers
- Worrying that if we let go of the memorabilia we'll lose the memories
- Agonising that we're not rich enough, good enough or clever enough

The list goes on. The point is that in stepping back we can let go of painful aspects of our past and move on to a new future. We can give our minds and souls permission to breathe deeply, as if for the first time. And we can begin to appreciate that we are not only loving beings, but loved and lovable, and that, with hope and courage, we can begin our own bright future.

I never see the point in starting the day with low spirits or in a sullen mood. This isn't always easy, but it's another choice. What right do I have to bring others down? Better to make a conscious effort to be cheerful and pleasant.

It has never been hard for me to see the glass half full, and in that I know I am lucky. I've had to battle through my life with people who struggle to see the glass as anything other than half empty and it has often been an uphill struggle bringing them on board with my plans. There have been times when I'd like to be getting on with the job in hand and instead I'm listening to objections, explaining, reassuring, soothing fears.

I've learned two things: first, there's no point in being defensive; and second, you can almost never change other people's minds if they're determined not to change. It's fine to have a discussion, or give an explanation, but when there's a fundamental disagreement there quickly comes a point where frustration sets in and the discussion becomes an argument.

There's a wonderful story in the Bible that sums up what I feel about negativity.

One day in the synagogue, Jesus healed a woman who had been crippled for eighteen years. Of course, the woman was overwhelmed with joy and she began to give thanks. But it happened to be the Sabbath, the holy day on which no work should be done, and there were some in the synagogue who condemned Jesus for healing the woman.

While the naysayers criticised and argued over the finer points of doctrine, the woman who had been healed continued to give thanks and praise God. She didn't stop to explain herself or try to convince the critics: she knew she couldn't change their minds. She simply kept on rejoicing and praising.

The woman could have stopped her rejoicing and started defending Jesus' actions, or tried to persuade the critics. But then the whole scene would have ended in a fight. Instead, by remaining thankful and continuing to praise, she created a wall of protection around herself. The critics left her alone and simply argued among themselves.

When people criticise, doubt, attack or undermine, it's often about them, not you. If you keep on doing what you're doing and refuse to engage with their waylaying tactics, they will keep on grumbling but you'll feel a lot better than if you stopped to argue with them. So the next time someone criticises something you're doing, just smile, try thanking them for their opinion and cheerfully carrying on.

I've met some young people who have been on our Leadership Academies at Columba 1400 and who have gone home full of hope and determination and ideas, only to be shot down by a disgruntled parent or friend. It's incredibly difficult to feel that you've found a way forward and then to have someone say something like, 'What makes you think you're special?' or 'You'll never manage that.' I feel disappointed when I hear about this kind of thing. Columba 1400 exists precisely to beat this kind of negativity. I always advise people who are the target of a negative reaction to endeavour to rise above it, refuse to take notice and carry on anyway. There are a whole host of Columban graduates who are now in good jobs, who have gained a college education or built a business of their own because they refused to be brought down by other people's negativity.

No doubt the negativity came from jealousy, or fear, or emotional pain, but while you can and should feel compassionate towards a person who apparently cannot escape this kind of negative attitude, it doesn't mean you have to listen to what they say and so be dragged down by them.

This is certainly true in business, management and industry. You've never truly led unless you've had someone come to you and dump their critical, complaining and negative views on you. I call it 'being sick all over you', because that's what it can feel like. And when it happens the temptation is to engage, to take it on board, to change what you're doing. A good leader should listen, surely? But while it's always right to listen to another viewpoint, it's also a good idea to think about what's going on for that person in the rest of their life; they may be behaving that way because they have personal issues or unfounded concerns. To get the best from people, you need to know them. And to truly lead, you need to balance your own goals for the business with the views of your colleagues and those for whom you are responsible. Yes, you should listen; but when you've resolved on a path, you should follow it through or you'll be led by the nose, rather than being true to yourself.

The wise attitude is to 'step back' before acting and think about why a particular person may be reacting in this way. It may be possible to head off a stream of criticism or complaint with kindness or concern about that person. See the person, not their words, tune out the negativity – but respond to the human need behind it.

One Christmas, when my son Christian was about seventeen, he asked for the DVD of the TV mini-series *Band of Brothers*. Great, we thought, that's one of the children's presents sorted.

He asked me if I would watch it with him on Boxing Day. I said I would. 'All of it, Dad – promise?' he said. I promised.

It was only on Christmas Day that I picked up the DVD box set and realised that the series was eleven hours long! I broke the news to Elizabeth. 'What?' she said. 'You'll be watching it all day!' I would, but I knew I had to keep my promise. Christian had thrown me a challenge, so early on Boxing Day he and I settled in front of the TV under our duvets, and began to watch.

It was a long day. We stopped for meal breaks but not much else, and the rest of the family had to carry on with Boxing Day without us.

Eventually we made it through the whole eleven hours, and although by the end I felt I'd watched enough TV for a lifetime, I did enjoy the story of Easy Company, the US Army's 101st Airborne Division and their mission on D-Day, 6 June 1944.

One of the things that stuck with me from *Band of Brothers*, apart from the comradeship and courage of the soldiers, was that anything or anyone not fit for core purpose – whether petty military regulations, excessive red tape, or thoughtless, selfish or bullying behaviour – was dismissed as 'chickenshit'. The term stayed with me and I now think of any pointless arguing, unkind comments, insistence on unnecessary rules and procedures, or anything else obviously small-minded as 'chickenshit'. Whenever I feel I'm being held back by this kind of thing I pause, 'step back' and think about how I can do things differently and refocus on what really matters.

Do what you feel in your heart to be right – for you'll be criticised anyway.

Eleanor Roosevelt, longest-serving
First Lady of the United States (1933–45)

Many things are impossible until they are done.

Nelson Mandela, first president of
South Africa to be elected by a
fully representative democratic process

6

Escape From Limitations

The human spirit is extraordinary. Its capacity for creativity, spiritual sustenance, endurance and hope is endless. As human beings we are immensely resilient and our spirits are capable of being continually reignited. This unique capability brings with it wonderful possibilities. So don't create limitations by seeing yourself as small, worthless, incapable or unimportant. Don't limit yourself to doing a reasonable job of things, or being merely competent. Think instead of your ability to rise to whatever is asked of you, to be far-sighted in handling any situation, to lead and inspire others. Because even if you have not yet seen these qualities in yourself, they are there.

The best way to discover for sure just how able you are, and how much you can achieve, is to step back for a while from the rush and hassle of your everyday commitments.

Our motto at Columba 1400 is a paraphrase of the timeless quote from great Scottish writer and statesman John Buchan: 'Our task is not to put the greatness back into humanity but to elicit it, for the greatness is there already.' Over and over again when people come to see me, we discover together that there is more in them than they think. I believe that this is true of all of us.

Through stepping back and taking time to really listen to yourself, to who you really are, you begin to care for your spirit and to realise that you are on a journey. Fresh perspectives appear from within and enable you to make sense of that which has been, and to move forward to that which might yet be, with greater clarity of direction and strength of purpose.

Sometimes in life we can feel as though we are simply going round in circles, but in truth life is always a pathway, however twisting and uncertain that pathway may appear. Mistakes and disappointments need not become major setbacks; they are simply steps along our way, and often the ones that lead to the greatest understanding and insight.

No matter what you feel your limits are, you can push beyond them. No matter what you have or have not achieved in your life so far, there is more, far more, that you can do. This is such an illuminating, exciting and enabling realisation. It is transformative. I see people's faces light up with the recognition of this truth, as a whole world of possibilities opens up.

To discover the great potential that you have within you, and to take in your stride whatever obstacles you encounter, you first need to accept and to love yourself. It is an essential truth that if you feel good on the inside, you can cope with anything that happens on the outside.

So what is it that makes us feel good inside? What gives us the aura that inner confidence brings? I think it's got a lot to do with having a sense of who we really are, and a feeling that who we really are is all right, no matter what anyone else may say or do. So many people feel that their lives are circumscribed by the expectations of others. They are oppressed by guilt and feelings of unworthiness, and live their lives according to what other people might think. How can you have confidence if you feel you're essentially wrong, bad or unacceptable? This applies to the rich and powerful and to the poor and disenfranchised alike: all of us have the same tendency to be defined by others' expectations; all of us need to break free from other people's limitations of us. To feel that the real you is not acceptable, that you must change or come across another way, is demoralising and diminishes us unjustly.

When you forgive yourself, when you let yourself be truly forgiven, you can let go of the past.

Let go of the Guard's Van

So many people are weighed down by the baggage of the past. They carry fear, shame, regret and guilt like millstones round their necks, and this takes away from the pleasure they might have in their lives. I often meet with outwardly successful men and women who are burdened by guilt and regret because they feel they have done something that they feel ashamed of – an adulterous affair, a hurtful act, a family break-up or a dubious business deal.

I call this the Guard's Van. There's an old film called *North West Frontier* in which the characters are taking a train across the desert. Kenneth More, playing the hero, is helping a small group of people to escape from a hostile situation in imperial India. But the train is too heavy to get away, so More's character unhooks the couplings which hold the guard's van to the rest of the train and lets it go. Unburdened, the train is able to accelerate smoothly and swiftly on to its destination.

So many of us need to let go of that Guard's Van we're dragging around. The sense of relief and freedom that letting go brings is immense.

When you accept and love yourself, you are able to trust your intuition – the most valuable resource you will ever have. Just as a theatre director or orchestra conductor knows how to direct, we have resources of knowledge that would inform our choices if we listened to our instincts. We all have a bank of experience on which to draw, but too often we don't trust ourselves.

Gather the facts and listen to what people have to say, by all means – but then, make your own decision, based on what your instinct tells you is right. We all have the capacity for wisdom and good judgement, but if we rely too much on the opinions of others we deny ourselves the chance to develop this capacity, whereas if we tap into it, and encourage and develop it, we come to trust our own judgement more and more. And if we are to find balance in all things, then we need to trust our judgement rather than always and only relying on the decisions and judgements of others.

To be OK with being OK is to be content with

yourself just the way you are. If we could all allow this sense to settle into our bones, we would find peace and goodwill.

When you develop this kind of inner confidence, it becomes a gift that you can pass on to others. One of the things we work hardest to do at Columba 1400 is to allow each young person who comes to us – generally from the 'tough realities' of life – to discover a sense of self, of who they are inside, and to realise who they are meant to be, and that is just fine. When all you've known is a home full of conflict, hurt and rejection it can be very hard to feel good about yourself.

We begin with the most basic things: a good meal, a safe, nurturing environment and a warm bed. Sometimes the simplest things are the most powerful. Just one person offering encouragement, interest and support can change someone's life. For many young people this interest means the difference between a life wasted and a life full of meaning and purpose. Look around you. Who is there that might benefit from your interest and encouragement?

Always look for the best in yourself and in others and you will be far more likely to find it. Of course, looking for the best in others sometimes means seeing past their current behaviour to the hidden depths of their potential. It means seeing past what *is* to what *might be*, and then encouraging and inspiring them so they can see that possible future for themselves.

There was a young boy who was constantly getting himself into trouble. He was a member of a local church youth club where the other boys got fed up with his noisy and disruptive antics and complained to the youth club leaders and their parents, who went to the parish minister and demanded that the boy be made to leave the club.

The parish minister thought about it and then said no, he would not throw the boy out. The minister knew the boy was a handful, but he saw a spark of something special in him and he refused to turn him away.

That young boy, Dougal Haston, grew up to be one of the greatest mountaineers Scotland has ever produced. Along with English climber Doug Scott, in an expedition led by Chris Bonnington, he was the first to reach the summit of Mount Everest by the south-west face in 1975, a route so dangerous that it hasn't been attempted since. There were many other climbing triumphs for Dougal, who became director of the International School of Mountaineering at Leysin in Switzerland. Like many who take great risks for their achievements, he died young: at the age of thirty-seven he was killed in an avalanche. Today there is a memorial to him in his birthplace, the parish of Currie, on the outskirts of Edinburgh.

By looking for the best you allow for the possibility of great things. When you expect failure, when you doubt yourself or those around you, when you are ready to give in at the first setback, then you shut down all the wonderful potential waiting to be unleashed, whereas by looking for the best, you open up to success, achievement, inspiration and moments of genius.

John Erskine, former professor of English at Columbia University, was an educator, concert pianist, author of sixty books, president of the Juilliard School of Music, and a popular and witty lecturer. Writing about his remarkable career, his wife Helen attributed it to what she called his defiant optimism. 'He was a good teacher', she said, 'because of his own excitement for learning and his trust in the future.' He would say to her, 'Let's tell our young people that the best books are yet to be written; the best paintings have not yet been painted; the best governments are yet to be formed; the best is yet to be done by them.'

We all have in us such great possibilities – the ability to cope with anything life throws at us. That's what the young carpenter from Nazareth meant when he said 'the kingdom of heaven is within you'. He was urging us not to look to outside forces for answers, but to look within ourselves. He always urged people to look for the best in themselves and in others. He told many wonderful stories, such as that of the Good Samaritan, not in order to give a new set of instructions to people about how to behave, but in order to inspire us to think differently about how we treat one another, and so challenge us about how we measure our own behaviour.

To do the best you can is not enough. You have to go out there and achieve what has to be achieved.
Winston Churchill, British prime minister during the Second World War

I failed over and over and over again in my life. And that is why I succeed.
Michael Jordan, American basketball player

7

Step Up

To step up means to go beyond what feels known, to push the boundaries, to make a big decision and then act on it. To achieve this will mean finding the most determined and motivated part of yourself, and mustering all your mental strength. It is sometimes easy to coast along, staying below the parapet, keeping your head down. You can reach a safe and comfortable level in work, in a relationship, in life, and then stay there.

Or you can step up to the next level, stick your neck out and be counted.

This will take courage and determination. It will mean drawing on your inner resources and being prepared to stand up for yourself and others and to think on your feet. It will mean that when there's a tough call, you face up to it rather than walking away.

If you want to be able to step up, though, you need to know yourself. So 'step back' for a period of reflection and self-monitoring. The self-monitoring I advocate is not about giving yourself a hard time, running through lists of 'I should have . . .' and 'Why didn't I . . . ?' That's all too easy to do, but not very valuable. You'll almost certainly feel worse when you've finished. Rather, the kind of self-monitoring I suggest is about setting your personal standards and being sure of making your own decisions. It's about self-knowledge. If you know yourself well, then you can make better choices.

To develop the habit of self-monitoring, take a little time out of the normal daily routine of your life, pause, reflect on where you are with your dreams and goals and ask yourself these questions:

- Am I being true to myself?
- Am I being honest with myself?
- Am I acting, at all times, with integrity?
- Have I been knocked off course somewhere?
- If so, what will help me to get back on course?
- Where do I fit in the picture of what is going on around me?

When you answer questions like these honestly and without self-blame, then you will be able to see yourself and your life clearly, and to make clear-headed decisions about the way forward. You'll also be able to see if there's something you need to change, to sort out, put right or re-evaluate. You can look again at what you love doing most and whether that's a significant enough part of your life; or at what you least enjoy and whether you can reduce this aspect of your life and work.

Don't let yourself be drawn into doing something that just isn't you simply because it sounds good, because you feel flattered, or because you're not very good at saying no. For me, engaging with people is hugely rewarding, and so is making positive decisions and then acting on them. I dislike sitting around in interminable meetings, having endless discussions and getting nowhere; that's just one of the reasons I have not gone into politics!

Break your goal down into stages, or bite-size chunks. Ask yourself, 'What can I manage that will make it feel possible to start?' Everything is easier taken in stages, and having a working plan helps too. Don't aim too low, but stretch yourself – aim for the biggest possible step up. As the motto of Gordonstoun School has it, *'Plus est en vous'* – there's more in you than you think.

Every time I've gone beyond what feels comfortable, I've felt afraid of what might happen; but no matter what the outcome, I've never regretted it. The more fearful you are, the more satisfying it will be when you succeed.

Be bold, be believable and, most of all, be brave

Sometimes the simplest way is to fool yourself and others by 'acting as if'; that is, to persuade yourself to feel motivated, courageous and clear, even if you don't actually feel those things at all. What's great is that when you act in a certain positive way, you begin to feel that way too. It's just the same as when you smile. Even if you didn't feel like smiling at all, a big smile will make you feel more cheerful, and it will certainly make others respond to you more warmly.

To step up often means having the courage of your convictions and being prepared to stand alone.

In 1955 Rosa Parks was arrested in Alabama for refusing to give up her seat on the bus to a white man. Boycotts and bloodshed followed, until the US Supreme Court ruled segregation unconstitutional. Rosa later wrote, 'Knowing what must be done does away with fear. When I sat down on the bus that day I had no idea history was being made, I was only thinking about getting home. But I had to make up my mind. After many years of being a victim . . . not giving up my seat, and whatever I had to face afterwards, wasn't important . . . I felt the Lord would give me the strength to endure whatever I had to face. It was time for someone to stand up, or in my case, sit down.'

When you can recover from disaster, disappointment and failure and carry on anyway, you develop resilience. And with resilience you can grasp opportunities and take risks. If we are afraid of things not working out, then we never try anything. Whereas if we are not afraid to fail, we'll keep on trying until we get it right, or it works out.

Doctor G. Campbell Morgan, a British evangelist and preacher and the pastor of Westminster Chapel in London in the early part of the twentieth century, told of a man whose shop burned to the ground. The next morning the man set up shop in the middle of the charred ruins and put up a sign that read, 'Everything lost except wife, children and hope – business as usual tomorrow morning.'

Small children have no fear of failure. They simply don't know the concept, until adults teach them. They happily try new things, fall over, laugh and try again. To fail teaches us something about ourselves. If we refuse the temptation to blame anyone or anything that comes to hand, we can find the lessons and the learning in every failure, and use it to become stronger and wiser.

When Benjamin Disraeli attempted to speak in parliament for the first time they booed him into silence. He said, 'Though I sit down now, the time will come when you will all hear me.' Disraeli became one of Britain's best orators and prime ministers. Today Disraeli's critics are forgotten, but his contribution to history lives on.

American inspirational author H. Jackson Brown gives two rules for winning:

> *Rule 1: Take one more step.*
> *Rule 2: When you can't take one more step, refer to rule number 1.*

It really is that simple. 'Step back' to reflect on where you are going and what you have learned, and then try again.

Sometimes it's just a question of doing something differently. Ralph Waldo Emerson, the nineteenth-century American essayist, lecturer and poet, tells a story of struggling while trying to wrestle a young calf into a barn. He was ready to give up when a young girl walked over to the calf and stuck her finger in its mouth. The calf, associating the sensation with its mother, followed the girl into the barn. What Emerson learned was that pushing and prodding doesn't work – for animals or people. But if you help people to feel secure, and that you can be trusted and they will benefit, they are likely to be far more amenable.

It can be the same with us. Sometimes, rather than just pushing ourselves up what may feel like an endless hill, we need to stop for inspiration, remembering just how much we can do and achieve when we know we're on the right path.

There are many wonderful examples of people who step up when the situation requires it. Where in your life do you need to step up, to conquer your fear of failure and come through, for yourself and for others around you?

'Step back' to look deep within yourself, find your reserves of courage and strength and then push beyond your limits.

*Are we going to work together, or are we just
going to have meetings?*

Peter Drucker, management consultant,
educator and author

*If you are here unfaithfully with us,
You're causing terrible damage.
If you've opened your loving to God's love
You're helping people you don't know and have
never seen.*

Rumi, Persian poet, theologian and Sufi mystic

8

Focus On What Matters

In regularly stepping back, we give ourselves a valuable opportunity to focus on what really matters in our lives.

We all get weighed down and distracted by 'stuff', most of which is unimportant in the grand scheme of things. It's easy to lose sight of what really matters when we're neck-deep in the 'stuff' that we feel we must take on. We begin to see the 'stuff' as vital, and to give less time and priority to the things that really are vital – such as health and family.

It's sometimes only when someone is facing the end of their life that the 'stuff' falls away and what truly matters shines clear and bright.

This was true of a good friend of mine, a talented and humorous Irishman named Shane O'Neill, whose life was tragically cut short. Shane was a very successful international financier and philanthropist, regarded by many as a potential senator in his native Ireland. He had worked long hours and made a lot of money. But when he was told he had a year to live, all his concerns were for his wife and three teenage children.

Shane was surrounded by people dealing with practical considerations when he called me to say, 'I want to talk to you about deep and lasting things.' I invited him and his wife Sheelagh to 'step back' for a weekend of quiet reflection at the beautiful Columba 1400 centre on the banks of Loch Lomond.

During that weekend Shane, by then very ill, summed up his working life with poignancy and wit by saying, 'My life has really been about two things – money and status. And when it wasn't about money and status, it was about status and money.'

Of course that wasn't entirely true, but the regret was deeply felt all the same.

How many people might say the same thing? And now, at the eleventh hour, Shane's sadness that he had not spent more time with his wife and children was acute. 'I wish I'd taught my children how to live,' he said. He was honest and courageous in his self-appraisal. And through that great courage and honesty he gave his children a lasting gift – he taught them how to die. He was a truly extraordinary man, who is much missed. His legacy lives on through his lovely wife Sheelagh and his equally remarkable children.

Shane found release and clarity in stepping back and appraising his life and the choices he'd made with such fearless honesty. In the headlong rush that life has become, we put off, delay and defer taking a long hard look at where we have chosen to focus our priorities, and whether it's time to make a change, but the fact is that most of us have the opportunity to do this long before we know that our days are numbered.

Charles Swindoll, a Texan pastor and founder of the Insight for Living radio broadcasts, writes in his book *Avoiding Stress Fractures*, 'I vividly remember sometime back being caught in the undertow of too many commitments and too few days. It wasn't long before I was snapping at my wife and our children, choking down my food at meal times, and feeling irritated at those unexpected interruptions through the day. Before long, things around our house started reflecting the pattern of my "hurry-up style". It was becoming unbearable. I distinctly recall after supper one evening the words of our younger daughter, Colleen. She wanted to tell me about something important that had happened to her at school that day. She hurriedly began "Daddy, I want to tell you something and I'll tell you really fast." Suddenly realising her frustration, I answered "Honey, you can tell me . . . and you don't have to tell me really fast, say it slowly." I'll never forget her answer: "Then listen slowly!"'

How many of us have been in that situation, or one that's similar? There are exchanges that are lost because we barely notice them, rushing a conversation – and in the process disappointing someone we love.

Children can be a wonderful guide in rediscovering how to focus. They know, unerringly, what really matters.

At an England versus New Zealand Test Match at Lord's Cricket Ground, a grandfather had set up his young grandson with a score book so as to score each and every ball of the first innings. This had been his practice when he was taken by his father to Lord's decades before. After a little while, the grandson turned to his grandfather and said, 'Grandad, after lunch can I give up scoring and watch the cricket?'

This story always makes me smile. The grandson knew that what mattered was simply to watch and enjoy the experience, not to keep the score.

Another way to focus one's mind is to endeavour to keep it grounded positively in the present. A simple yet effective way to achieve this is to recite a daily 'mantra'. The following Sanskrit proverb is one of my favourites.

Look to this day . . .
For yesterday is but a dream
And tomorrow is only a vision.
But today well lived
Makes every yesterday
A dream of happiness
And every tomorrow
A vision of hope.
Look well therefore to this day.
Such is the salutation of the dawn.

To focus is to get to the core of the issue. What matters to me, and what do I need to do about it?

Keep it simple and avoid overstrategising. This isn't about creating a plan or a list or a model. It's simply a question of looking into your heart and recognising that there are some things that matter much more than others, and then asking yourself if you reflect that in the way you live.

Leonard Cohen put to music a poem by Canadian poet Frank Scott called 'Villanelle of our Time':

From bitter searching of the heart,
Quickened with passion and with pain
We rise to play a greater part.

This is the faith from which we start:
Men shall know commonwealth again
From bitter searching of the heart.

Do you care for yourself, for your family and friends, for your staff, associates and colleagues?

It's worth asking yourself if, as you run from one thing to another, time is wasted that might be better spent. Take meetings as an example. Especially when badly chaired, they can be a terrible waste of time. A group of people can spend hours sitting around a table talking and getting nowhere, when a few brief, clear and honest one-to-one conversations would solve everything. Meetings can too often be full of checklists, and they seldom inspire and enable people. Bring your head and your heart together, keep your humanity and try a new approach; cut through the bureaucracy and get to the core of what needs to be done.

A survey of people leaving a job or retiring asked, 'What do you wish you had done more of?' The overwhelming response was, 'I wish I had spent more time with people, one on one.' Listen to yourself, and listen to others too. Who is trying to tell you something that you need to hear?

To focus is to clear the pathway forward, to act with integrity and openheartedness and to bring new light to what needs to be addressed.

When you 'step back' and focus on what matters, you begin to see the small stuff for what it is, and that can be immensely liberating. You renew your inner energy, you rediscover hope and joy, you allow yourself to feel human and fully alive and authentic, and you regain your alertness, mental agility and sense of perspective.

The One Thing all famous authors, world class athletes, business tycoons, singers, actors and celebrated achievers in any field have in common is that they all began their journeys when they were none of these things.

Mike Dooley, former tax consultant, speaker and author of *Notes from the Universe*

Sometimes it is the people no one imagines anything of who do the things that no one can imagine.

From the film *The Imitation Game*, the story of code-breaker Alan Turing

9

Overcome Failure

What so often holds us back is the fear of failure. And yet every single person alive fails at something at some point. Things go wrong; it is part of the human condition, and it's the way we learn and move forward.

Which of us has set out on any venture, large or small, without a few setbacks along the way?

We all make errors of judgement and find things going 'pear-shaped' from time to time, but if we don't let them stop us, our setbacks can give us our greatest opportunities for learning.

I've made plenty of mistakes over the years, some small, some big. And I've had setbacks which have threatened to derail everything I set out to do. But the way I see it, why would I let anything, however difficult it might be, prevent me from carrying on? If you learn from failure, you take a step towards success. Only when you accept failure as final are you finally a failure.

When failure looms, or things go wrong, that is the time to step back and re-evaluate what is going on. His Holiness the Dalai Lama, a wonderfully humorous and generous man, once said, 'Remember that not getting what you want is sometimes a wonderful stroke of luck.' I am often reminded of how true this is. From the ashes of our failures and setbacks come our greatest joys and successes.

But that is less likely to be true if our reaction to failures, upsets and misfortunes is to run around like headless chickens or, conversely, to freeze and do nothing. Either way, the problem only gets worse.

When things get uncomfortable and people around you are banging their fists on the table (literally or metaphorically), making threats or panicking, then keep absolutely calm, step back – even if only for a moment – and think through what's happening. This is something which I learned to do from my father at an early age. He always said, 'Whatever happens, don't panic.' I've always used this approach. The hotter and more fraught or worrying things get, the quieter and calmer I appear. I may not feel that way inside, in fact I may well be churned up, but I've found time and time again that to slow down and behave calmly is the best course of action. It has a soothing effect on those around you and it gives you time to think out a course of action.

It's invariably the people who hang in there who see failure as a step on the road to success. It was author and philosopher Paulo Coelho who said in his book *The Alchemist*, 'The secret of life is to fall seven times and to get up eight times.' Get back up every time you fall, because one of those times will be the last – you will succeed.

I believe that if you stick at something long enough and with enough momentum, then you can't help but succeed. Perseverance is everything. It is certainly the difference between failure and success in most endeavours. If you get knocked back, if your attempt to make changes doesn't seem to be working, if your suggestions or requests seem to fall on deaf ears, then pause, take a breath, gather your strength and persevere. You will be so very glad that you did.

Jonas Salk, the American medical researcher and virologist who discovered the polio vaccine, had a great attitude. He said, 'Everything that you do is, in a sense, succeeding. It's telling you what not to do as well as what to do. Not infrequently, I go into the laboratory and people say something didn't work. And I say "Great, we've made a great discovery." If you thought it was going to work, and it didn't work, that tells you as much as if it did. So my attitude is not one of pitfalls; my attitude is one of challenges and "what is nature telling me".'

Such tenacity is the hallmark of all committed and successful people. They keep trying, keep learning and keep moving forward. They win the battle in their minds and then it overflows into what they do.

Sometimes we trip up through inexperience, doubt or questions that others throw at us, but when we do we have a choice. We can feel we've been dealt an unfair hand, we can curse and blame and ultimately give up, or we can decide to put things right, overcome obstacles and get back on track.

Blaming and complaining are a waste of time. No one feels better for it and nothing changes. Better instead to sort the situation out, change what needs changing and build trust and confidence.

Stepping back can provide the space for renewal – of energy, of intention and of your ability to see clearly. When things get difficult, step back and do something that makes you happy. A little time out to enjoy a walk, a film or a talk with a friend will help you to get back on track and pick up the baton again.

Sir James Dyson, famed British inventor, entrepreneur and engineer, took his idea for developing a bagless vacuum cleaner to many multinational companies. They all rejected it. It took fifteen years of frustration, perseverance, and over five thousand prototypes, not to mention heavy debt, before he finally launched the Dyson DCO1 bagless cleaner under his own name. Within eighteen months it became the best-selling cleaner in the UK. Today Dysons are sold in over fifty countries and in the UK one in three of us owns a Dyson.

If you constantly berate yourself, or allow yourself to feel that you can't get anything right, then you will grind to a halt. Ultimately you can't do anything of worth unless you are OK about being OK. It's the cornerstone of a positive attitude. Keep your feet on the ground but like yourself at the same time, acknowledge that you're doing your best and accept that this is OK.

If you have self-belief you don't blame others when things go wrong. You take responsibility for whatever choices you have made – and there are always choices; the phrase 'I had no choice' is often spoken but very seldom true. We are not helpless beings, we have free will and the opportunity to make our own decisions.

As the great French philosopher, writer and political activist Jean Paul Sartre said, 'We are our choices.' And we can make the choice to cope, to stay calm and to carry on.

It's also useful, when contemplating failure, to consider what you mean by success. What is it that you are working towards, hoping for or trying to create? Sometimes our ideas about success are limited, as this lovely story illustrates.

Writing in the *Globe and Mail*, a Toronto newspaper, Joanna Norland described her frustrations with her squirmy, dreamy eight-year-old son Josh. A high-achiever herself, Joanna wanted Josh to excel and to ace all his tests. She drilled him with tables, spelling tests and writing exercises, but while Josh was keen to do well, he was easily distracted and no matter how hard his mother pushed him, his work was littered with mistakes. Then came the afternoon of the school sports day. As Josh lined up for the 600-metre track race, his mother hoped that maybe this time he would finally beat his rivals. The race began and one of the other children stumbled and fell. 'Ha,' thought Joanna, 'a chance to outpace the competition. Go Josh!'

That's when Josh stopped in his tracks, retraced his steps and held out his hand to pull his buddy back to his feet. His classmates cheered as Josh rounded his final lap and his mother ran to give him a hug. As she wrote in her article, 'Warm, friendly, empathetic. Not empty placeholders after all, but the foundations for a worthwhile life.'

Josh's success lay in his ability to connect with others, to care and to respond. These are not quantifiable 'successes' as his school subjects would be, but they matter a whole lot more.

So when you step back, use the time to reflect on what success means to you, and what you hope to achieve.

Be prepared to rise to any challenge you are set, and to handle any situation, no matter how difficult or demanding.

Step back each day, and choose your attitude for the day, every day. Choose to feel good about yourself and to bring smiles to the faces of the people you encounter. Choose to be patient, understanding, kind and supportive, to yourself and to those around you. Choose to take failure in your stride.

Failure is a gift, because life is all about how you cope with your failures. It says a lot more about you than your successes. If you fail, forgive yourself, sort the problem if you can, get back up and move on, without blaming anyone else or feeling sorry for yourself. Horrible, difficult things happen to everyone and it can feel miserable and defeating, especially if it's a big setback. But it will only be as big as you let it be. Shrink it to pin-size in your mind and then carry on.

If you step back and take time for reflection, it's extraordinary how solutions present themselves.

Experience is not what happens to you; it's what you do with what happens to you.

Aldous Huxley (1894–1963), novelist, author of *Brave New World*

We must accept finite disappointment, but never lose infinite hope.

Martin Luther King, activist and civil rights leader

10

Take Stock – And Then Keep Going

I am a great believer in hanging in there when things get difficult. So if you feel that life is throwing up obstacles and you're losing sight of your end goal, then 'step back', take a little time out, and take stock. It may feel like slowing down when you think you should be speeding up, but in fact it will help you immeasurably to move forward again in a more productive and enlightened way.

Stepping back in such circumstances will help you to see potential difficulties as opportunities rather than obstacles. It will give you the space to see a way round, and to be convinced anew that you should never stop trying, but instead can learn from everything that comes your way and prove to everyone, yourself included, just what you can do. Taking stock is not a cop-out – it's the way to rediscover your conviction to keep going.

We all have tough times, when we just don't have the answers. That's when the wise and the brave and the determined just keep on going.

If you believe in yourself and in what you are doing, then giving up is simply not an option. Not that it isn't tempting to chuck the whole thing in at times – whether that's a job, a relationship, a project, a sporting or artistic challenge, or a business opportunity. When you feel down, uncertain, rejected and hurt, when giving up seems like the only choice, it takes real courage to keep going and do it anyway.

There's a lovely story about one of the world's greatest violinists. When asked as an old man why he still practised between six and eight hours every day, he replied, 'Because I think I'm getting better.' I believe that if you stick at something long enough and with enough momentum, then you can't help but succeed. Perseverance is everything. It is certainly the difference between failure and success in most endeavours. If you get knocked back, if your attempts to make changes don't seem to be working, if your suggestions or requests fall on deaf ears or you don't feel that you're getting anywhere, then pause, 'step back', take a breath, gather your strength – but persevere. You will be so very glad that you did.

Disappointment and setbacks can be painful, but that needn't mean you're wrong. The important thing is not to let them stop you. Lick your wounds, get back up and try again.

> Sir Harry Lauder was a well-known and much-loved music hall entertainer before and during the First World War. He entertained the troops and was knighted for raising over a million pounds to help servicemen return to health and civilian life.
>
> Sir Harry was playing in London in 1916, just before Christmas, when he received a telegram to say that his only son, Captain John Lauder of the Argyll and Sutherland Highlanders, had been killed in action at Pozières. That night he put aside his grief and he went on stage and played to a packed house. Later, in the wake of his son's death, he wrote the song 'Keep Right on to the End of the Road' which includes the lines, 'Tho' the way be long, let your heart be strong . . . tho' you're tired and weary, still journey on.'

There's a passage written by US president Theodore Roosevelt for a speech he gave at the Sorbonne in Paris in 1910 which, for me, sums up the importance and the value of throwing yourself into the fray, being a participant in life, not a bystander, and keeping going, no matter what the challenges or hurdles.

> *It's not the critic who counts;*
> *not the man who points out how the strong man*
> *stumbles,*

*or where the doer of deeds could have done them
better.*

*The credit belongs to the man who is actually in the
arena,*

whose face is marred by dust and sweat and blood;

*who strives valiantly; who errs, who comes short
again and again,*

*because there is no effort without error and
shortcoming;*

but who does actually strive to do the deeds;

who knows great enthusiasms, the great devotions;

who spends himself in a worthy cause;

*who at the best knows in the end the triumph of
high achievement,*

*and who at the worst, if he fails, at least fails while
daring greatly,*

*so that his place shall never be with those cold and
timid souls*

who neither know victory nor defeat.

We're all on a journey, and we can get so focused on the immediate future, the next step or two, that we forget it's really about the long road, the road we have already travelled and the road that lies ahead, into the future.

Each time you 'step back', it's important to think about how you are doing in the light of that big picture, where it's working and what you should celebrate. It's also important to appreciate the small, seemingly unimportant things which you so often take for granted. By stepping back regularly, you can appreciate the journey and where you have come from.

Stepping back gives you the clarity of vision to see that the long road is about continuing with your journey, wherever it may take you, until you have achieved what you set out to do. The long road is about looking back, and looking forward: looking back to enjoy how far we have come, and to remind ourselves of the lessons we have learned; and looking forward to relish what is yet to come, to develop and to improve.

When I look back, I look at what I did right, what worked, what was good that I could use again, which ideas are worth renewing, which approach to problem-solving worked, who helped with what and whether that is the role they're best suited to. I look for all that is good and useful, let go of what isn't, and carry the best along with me for the future.

When I look ahead, I try to be realistic, to think about what could go wrong, and prepare for it, because few things ever run smoothly all the way through. It's not that I want events or people to fail, but I hope not to be caught out by unpleasant surprises. Of course, I hope and pray that things won't go wrong, but with any major undertaking there are always a few glitches – small ones if you're lucky but sometimes larger, and quite likely through no fault of your own – and it's best to be ready for them. So when I'm planning I try to factor in extra time, money, help or back-up if possible.

This careful planning doesn't stop me from starting out on any venture with motivation and determination, and with the inner conviction that what I am doing is going to work.

What is it you are waiting to do? What vision do you want to make into a reality? It might be joining an evening class, starting a business, setting off on a journey or learning a language. It might be changing your job for something potentially more exciting and satisfying, or doing some voluntary work with a group of people you care about. Or it might be prioritising your relationship, spending more time with your children, or cutting back your working hours. The chances are that it's something you've been thinking about for a while, carrying it around in the back of your mind, planning to do something about it, perhaps, one day, maybe.

Do it now. Take the first small step, and plan another and another after that. When you stop waiting or finding all the reasons to hold back, you feel empowered. When I talk to people who are hesitant, dissatisfied, bored or simply aware that they need change in their lives, I always encourage them to take time to 'step back'. Out of that space will come answers, energy and creativity.

One day some young people arrived on Skye in a mini-bus, on their way to Columba 1400. Not knowing the way, the driver took some wrong turns and got lost. He eventually stopped to ask an old crofter if he knew the way and the old man, slowly taking the pipe from his mouth, looked at the driver for a minute or so and then said, 'Ye cannae get there frae here.' At that point a young voice piped up from the back of the minibus, 'Yes you can, you can get anywhere from here.'

And you can. From where you are today, whatever the circumstances of your life, you can get to wherever you choose to go.

Some tasks can seem enormous. It can seem too daunting – easier, perhaps, not to even try. But the answer is encapsulated in a Chinese proverb which says, 'It is better to light a candle than to curse the darkness.' In other words, in whatever way your life is unsatisfactory, it's time to change it. Start somewhere, with one action which will make a difference. Even if your goal is as ambitious as world peace, you can start by making peace with a neighbour, being alongside a friend in need, or giving a few hours to helping out at a local charity or another cause dear to your heart.

Faith is an oasis in the heart which will never be reached by the caravan of thinking.

Khalil Gibran, Lebanese poet and author

We need to find God, and he cannot be found in noise and restlessness.
God is the friend of silence.
See how nature – trees, flowers, grass – grows in silence;
see the stars, the moon and the sun, how they move in silence.
We need silence to be able to touch souls.

Mother Teresa of Calcutta

11

Have Faith

We live in an increasingly busy age, a 24-hour-a-day world, dominated by technology and material success, in which the focus is always outwards. And yet we still search for a spiritual dimension, and for meaning and purpose in our lives.

It is only in the peace and stillness of stepping back that we begin to find answers to our spiritual questions and have the opportunity to connect with our own personal faith.

In stepping back, in quietness and reflection, we can begin to feel an inner, deeper power or presence that brings a sense – even in dark and difficult times – that there is more to life than our present troubles. At moments like these faith can be discovered or renewed: faith in the future, in hope and in ourselves.

To have faith is to believe and to trust. For some of us, to believe in our own ability and in the love of those around us seems enough, while for others faith extends beyond us to a higher power. For me, faith has always been the mainstay of my life. My view of faith is open, inclusive and tolerant. The Bible teaches kindness and a loving and forgiving heart, and Jesus' many acts of kindness are an example to all. Other religions share this belief in the power of kindness. When the Dalai Lama says, 'My religion is kindness,' I think, 'Yes: me too.' It is said that the Torah, the central set of books in the Jewish tradition, begins and ends with acts of kindness. The Qur'an, the central religious text of Islam, advocates the virtue of kindness, and Hindu scriptures also advocate kindness and speak of kindness as purification. The other living religions of the world, Sikhism, Shintoism, Jainism, Zorastrianism, Taoism and Confucianism, also have kindness as a central belief or principle.

I believe that all true seekers will come to the same source; and of course all religions share the same beliefs in inherent goodness and the golden rule to love your neighbour as you love yourself. Mainstream faiths, at their best, encourage people towards simplicity of living, positivity of outlook and kindness.

I am a minister of the Church of Scotland, but I've never seen the Church as a club where you have to behave well in order to get into it, or Jesus as the leader of a sect. We know historically that Jesus lived, and that he went about doing good. For myself, I start from that simple basis and try to follow his example. This results in a sense of purposeful well-being and feeling accompanied by a spiritual sense of God's presence.

I can't agree with the narrow, unforgiving, judgemental attitudes of certain religious groups who condemn others or whose preaching perpetuates intolerance, misunderstanding and, worst of all, violence. I believe it is our differences that make us strong and we should delight in them. There's a wonderful adaptation of a famous prayer written by St Thérèse of Lisieux, a young Carmelite nun who died when she was only twenty-four, but who had great wisdom and who urged self-acceptance and the forgiveness of faults:

> May today there be peace within. May you trust that you are exactly where you are meant to be. May you not forget the infinite possibilities that are born of faith in yourself and others. May you use the gifts that you have received and pass on the love that has been given to you. May you be content with yourself just the way you are. Let this knowledge settle into your bones and allow your soul the freedom to sing, dance, praise and love. It is there for each and every one of us.

With faith – in yourself, in your goal, in your beliefs – extraordinary things are possible. Faith gives us hope, even when a situation seems hopeless. It is faith that allows us to feel compassion and kindness towards others and to forgive those who hurt us, because we are aware of the essential drive towards goodness in the human soul, and because we know that grudges, which can spoil many lives, are just too heavy to carry.

Gordon Wilson was a shopkeeper in Enniskillen, Northern Ireland, a quiet, modest and very private man. On Remembrance Sunday 1987, Gordon went with Marie, aged twenty-one, the youngest of his three children, to join the ceremony at the town's cenotaph. Moments later Gordon and Marie, a nurse, were caught in an IRA bomb blast. Trapped under the rubble of a collapsed building, Gordon found Marie's hand. 'Daddy, I love you,' she told him. She didn't speak again, and when they were rescued Gordon learned that Marie had died. Heartbroken at the loss of his child and with a badly injured arm, Gordon returned home to grieve quietly with his wife. Not long afterwards a BBC reporter knocked on his door to ask him how he felt about the people who had killed his daughter. Gordon said, 'I bear no ill will, I bear no grudge.'

Gordon's call for forgiveness and reconciliation came to be called 'the Spirit of Enniskillen' and was referred to by The Queen in her Christmas Day message that year. Gordon went on to become a peace campaigner, urging both sides in the Irish troubles to accept one another and end hostilities.

Gordon Wilson didn't set out to be an example, but his sense of forgiveness, born of his deep faith, proved an inspiration to many others. Even in the agony of his loss, he was able to 'step back' from the impulse to hate and see the bigger picture.

The wise and mysterious poet and author Khalil Gibran wrote, 'Out of suffering have emerged the stronger souls; the most massive characters are seared with scars.' How true it is that those who have suffered most can very often be of most help and inspiration to others.

In 2000, South Korea's president Kim Dae-jung, a man of great faith, courage and fortitude, was awarded the Nobel Peace Prize for his 'sunshine policy' towards North Korea. By means of warmth and friendliness he sought to lay the foundations for a peaceful reunification of the two Korean states, which had been in a state of war since 1950.

It was not only Kim Dae-jung's policy of reconciliation with the neighbouring state to the north that the Nobel Committee set store by. It also valued his long and courageous struggle for democracy and human rights in his own country, which had entailed long periods of imprisonment, house arrest, kidnapping and exile.

In the summer of 2000, Kim Dae-jung arranged a summit meeting with North Korea's leader, one result of which was that family members who had been separated for over forty years were allowed to meet. South

Korea maintained its humanitarian aid to its neighbour, and relations between the two have since developed in the fields of transport, sports, art and culture.

If we all adopted a 'sunshine policy' towards those who antagonise and hurt us, how much more peace and goodwill there would be in the world – and how much more good health, because it is a medical certainty that forgiveness adds years to your life.

Begin your reflective practice, make it a regular part of your life, and it will bring you into a deeper relationship with that higher power, wherever you may be on your journey of faith. The process of inner discovery might take time; it might not happen the first day. Stick with it. Faith is there for you to find. You can feel connected to it in all kinds of situations – on a hillside, when a child is born, looking out to sea, as well as in a church or a holy place; these are often good, quiet places to start.

My father loved to go to church. It was where he 'recharged his batteries', and that's why he went as regularly as he did. He enjoyed the peace and the spiritual inspiration and felt enriched by it. That was his way of stepping back and as the years have gone by, I have come to appreciate his wisdom.

For me, stepping back in nature gives me great joy, and I think of prayer as an activity that can be part of everything else I am doing. Not long ago I went for a long walk on the Isle of Skye, the place in which I am always at my happiest. It was a lovely crisp winter day and I walked round the Dun, the old Pictish fort, close by our home at the north end of the island. My spirit felt filled with the peace and beauty of the day and I couldn't help praying with joy and gratitude.

He who cares for his own child is like a stream
which nourishes a tree along its banks.
But he who loves another's child is like a cloud
which goes from the sea into the desert
and waters there a lonesome tree.

The Talmud

Be a rainbow in someone else's cloud.
Maya Angelou, author and poet,
in *Letter to my Daughter*

12

Make A Difference

I believe that it is what we do for others that gives our lives true meaning and purpose. People come alive when they are doing good. I believe that if this is one thing you focus on in life, then you will find fulfilment and joy. When, on behalf of others, we give energy and intent, we let light into our own lives and uncover the great potential that is buried within each of us. It's like being a small child who wakes to a bright morning and rubs the sleep from his eyes, full of wonder. 'Step back' and think about where in the situation you are starting from; you can make a positive impact on the lives of others and give without the expectation of profit or return. It is something we all need. Without this, life is two-dimensional, flat, dull and precarious – the two-legged stool which inevitably overbalances and falls over.

According to the influential twentieth-century American economist J. K. Galbraith, people think about themselves on average every forty-five seconds. If you're a two-minute person, that's exceptional. Of course, there's nothing wrong with thinking about ourselves and none of us can help doing it, but it's a good idea to focus a bit less on yourself and a bit more on others.

We live in a time that's all about 'me'. There are great aspects to this – we have more rights and we are more aware of the rights we have; we are less likely to be put down or treated badly or cheated without fighting back; and we have become accustomed to having our say and are therefore better at speaking up. But there's a point beyond which too much 'me' gets tiresome and unhealthy. St Francis of Assisi, the spoiled son of an Italian nobleman, who gave up his heritage to serve others, wrote, 'It is by forgetting oneself that one finds self.' That's when putting the 'me' aspect aside in order to focus on others is the best way forward. Often when addressing audiences at meetings and conferences, I say in reference to our Columba 1400 core values that 'in self-forgetfulness lies self-fulfilment', and it always evokes a heartfelt response; it is something of which people like to be reminded. There is a great focus these days on finding oneself, discovering a deeper under-standing of the self. This is no bad thing. We need to understand ourselves, our motivations and our hopes and dreams – but the route to finding oneself isn't just through introspection.

To contribute to the lives of others in this way is not a chore or drudgery or a burden – rather, it is freedom. To me there is nothing greater than the sheer excitement and joy of being of use and service in this world. It is my core purpose, running through my life like the writing at the centre of a stick of rock. Increasingly I discover the pleasure and relief of putting myself to one side, and of listening to and focusing on others.

Sometimes, at social gatherings, you see people who are so keen to tell their own stories that neither side of the conversation is really listening. If you let go of the need to get your story across and just listen, it can be enriching and enabling. It's a bit like a walkie-talkie. If it's constantly on 'send', then it can't 'receive'. Switch your own transmitter to 'receive' so you can hear what others need, and you will find a way to make genuine and lasting connections with others.

William Gladstone and Benjamin Disraeli were great leaders and intense rivals. Gladstone, leader of the Liberal Party, is considered by many to personify the best qualities of Victorian England. A career public servant, he was a great orator, master of finance and a staunchly moral man. He was made prime minister of Great Britain on four separate occasions, the only person in history to achieve such an honour. Under his leadership, Great Britain established a national education system, instituted parliamentary reform and saw the vote given to a significant number of people in the working classes.

Disraeli, who served as prime minister twice, had a different kind of background. In his thirties he entered politics and built a reputation as a diplomat and social reformer. His greatest accomplishment was masterminding Britain's purchase of the Suez Canal.

Both men accomplished much. But what really separated them was their approach to people – a difference best illustrated by a story told by a young woman who happened to dine with each of the two rival statesmen on consecutive evenings.

When asked for her impression of them she said, 'When I left the dining room after seeing Mr Gladstone, I thought he was the cleverest man in England. But after sitting next to Mr Disraeli, I thought I was the cleverest woman in England.'

There are so many ways in which we can make a difference; it isn't just a question of doing some specific useful or kind act for someone else – desirable though that is. It can be changing something for the better, such as making the workplace a more pleasant environment or speaking up for someone who needs support, enabling someone to fulfil their potential, or even stopping someone from making a move in the wrong direction.

In 1863 a Jesuit priest by the name of Father Strickland is recorded as saying, 'A man may do an immense deal of good, if he does not care who gets the credit for it.' Over the years this saying has been appropriated by many great men and women in history and the generally recognised modern equivalent is, 'There is no limit to what a person can do if he or she doesn't mind who gets the credit.' Both versions encapsulate the secret of making a difference and enabling others, without looking for credit. Creating achievements is enough, without needing to keep a tally of who did what or who deserves the glory. To contribute in this way puts you in the background, and by doing so it releases you to stop worrying about how you will look or focusing on what's in it for you. As the ancient Greeks put it, 'A society grows great when old men plant trees under whose shade they know they shall never sit.'

Thinking about and giving to others makes us happy. It's a win-win! The search for that elusive thing we call happiness can be over, once you stop looking for it and worrying about it and decide to roll your sleeves up and get busy on behalf of someone else.

His Holiness the Dalai Lama puts it like this:

I believe that the very purpose of life is to be happy. From the very core of our being, we desire contentment. In my own limited experience I have found that the more we care for the happiness of others, the greater is our own sense of well-being. Cultivating a close, warm-hearted feeling for others automatically puts the mind at ease. It helps remove whatever fears or insecurities we may have and gives us the strength to cope with any obstacles we encounter. It is the principal source of success in life. Since we are not solely material creatures, it is a mistake to place all our hopes for happiness on external development alone. The key is to develop inner peace.

The search for material satisfaction is endemic in our society. So many of us believe that bigger, better, newer and flashier means happier. And when it doesn't we redouble our efforts. But as the Dalai Lama says, 'We are not solely material creatures; we need to fulfil our spiritual dimension, to find inner peace, and the path to this is to care for others.' In other words, in order to gain more depth internally, we need to give more.

In my coaching work I see people of every age and from every walk of life. Sometimes there will be business leaders who, in the race to compete and make a profit, have lost their way, forgotten who they are and have realised they want life to be about more than just work. Often it's a question of opening their eyes to the hopes and dreams and plans they can still pursue, not to enhance their own coffers, but to help others.

When a highly regarded international businessman went to visit Mother Teresa in the Missionaries of Charity hostel where she, with the other nuns, nursed the sick and the poor, he was keen to explain to her all he had achieved. Mother Teresa listened patiently. When he had finished she said to him, 'And what do you do that matters?'

I call that a 'spring-cleaning' question. The kind that makes you stop, think and re-evaluate just about everything in your life and ask yourself, 'What can I do to make a difference?'

Young people setting out in their working lives come to me because they are seeking meaning and purpose in their careers. People who feel their jobs have reached a dead end come to me because they don't want to stay in that job all their lives. Just like the business leaders, they all need to find meaning somewhere – and they have realised that their day job just isn't enough.

You can find meaning and purpose in a job, as many people do. But sometimes the meaning and purpose of life lies not so much in the job but in something else – a commitment to helping a local youth and community club, to visiting the sick or to cleaning up the local nature reserve. What's right for you depends on who you are and what matters most to you. But the questions are the same:

Are you contributing to the community around you?
Do you have a sense of purpose?
What can you do to make a difference?

Never mistake making money for making a difference: they are not the same. Step outside your usual routines, let go of 'What's in it for me?' and go out and change something: find a voice, be influential, stand up for the oppressed. Take the decision to make a difference and have a positive impact on the lives of others.

What drives that impulse to be of use is the spirit of love. There's a wonderful quote from Henry Drummond, namesake but regrettably no relation, who was the first Professor of Science and Religion at the University of Edinburgh in 1880. He said, 'When you look back on your life you will discover that the times you felt most fully human and alive were the times when you were acting in a spirit of love.' His words appeared in *The Greatest Thing in the World*, a book based on his address on 1 Corinthians 13, St Paul's great hymn of love. The book was a bestseller at the time, second only to the Bible, and it still remains a marvellous read to this day.

To lead your life with the spirit of love at its core doesn't mean you have to be a saint, to get everything right, to be always loving and kind and never fall down. But it does mean you try to achieve loving-kindness, compassion, concern and interest towards others. It means choosing the peaceful path rather than conflict, and it means letting go of ego and of the need to be right.

Booker T. Washington was part of the last generation of black American leaders born into slavery and became the leading voice of the former slaves and their descendants. As an African-American educator, author, orator and adviser to successive presidents of the United States he was, between 1890 and 1915, the foremost leader in the African-American community. He was a man of incredible courage and determination, and the core tenets of his lifelong philosophy were 'Character is power' and 'If you want to lift yourself up, lift up someone else'.

When you give generously, from the heart, without expectation, it's extraordinary how the blessings come back to you. Small acts of kindness radiate rays of goodwill like sunshine and bring kindness back into your life in other ways.

In a study conducted by Harvard Medical School and published in December 2008 in the *British Medical Journal*, four classes of Harvard students were followed from just before the Second World War in 1939 to the present day. The findings of the study discovered that happiness depends on emotional intelligence, skill at human relationships, joy, connection, resilience and the ability to give to others. True life fulfilment, they found, is about human relationships and giving to others. What's more, if you are fulfilled, you can expect to live longer – the study found that there is a clear connection between this fulfilment, based on relationships and the ability to give, and life expectancy. A warm, loving family, one of the research team said, is more important than a trust fund or a title.

So the ability to give to others is directly linked to happiness and to longer life. What could be more perfect?

In his early days Nelson Mandela was motivated by a dream to free himself from oppression, but his dream expanded to include others.

> The hunger for my own freedom became the greater hunger for the freedom of my people. It was this desire for freedom of my people to live their lives with dignity and self-respect that animated my life, that transformed a frightened young man into a brave one, that drove a law-abiding attorney to become a criminal, that turned a family-loving man into a man without a home, that forced a life-loving man to live like a monk.

When Mandela found himself at a crossroads in life – with one path leading to personal gain and the other to serving his people – he chose the more difficult road of helping others.

Being confronted with that decision in our own lives does not mean abandoning our dreams. It means expanding them. This is a journey we can take together.

If you do not change direction, you may end up where you are heading.

Lao Tzu, ancient Chinese philosopher

Part 2
The Many Ways
of Stepping Back

The benefits of stepping back from your usual routine cannot be overstated. Our minds are like computers and just as computers need to switch off and reboot sometimes, so too do our minds. And for this rebooting to be truly effective, we need solitude and silence.

Most of us are not used to silence. Many of us find silence, even for brief periods, uncomfortable and unnatural. In fact it is the most natural thing possible, but we live in a world where the sound of silence has been drowned out by a cacophony of constant noise, much of which is jarring and disturbing to the soul.

So it is worth overcoming the resistance you may feel to stopping. We have lots of reasons for this resistance: 'I can't fit it in', 'I can't afford to stop', 'I don't have time', 'I'll get around to it soon', or 'It's not really my kind of thing'. I've heard these and many more similar protests dozens of times. But busy people the world over can and do make space for peace, for reflection, for putting demands aside and allowing the light of creativity in – and they flourish as a result.

Finding peace of mind is not a strenuous job, though; it is a calm and gentle process. And when there is peace inside you, that peace permeates to the outside of you too. It spreads around you, so that others sense it, and they too can benefit.

Make A Start

The only way to make space in your life on a regular basis, I've discovered, is to plan it. You can't wait for it to come along. 'I'll think about it when I have a quiet afternoon' is just not going to work. You need to put space into your diary, just as you need to put in times for exercise, or it won't happen.

That said, if you find the thought of spending some time in complete silence feels too daunting, then begin your stepping back in small ways, with a change of scene, peaceful music, gentle activity. Gradually, as you discover the benefits, you will reach a point where you can feel comfortable with silence and ultimately you will come to feel that periods of silence are vital to your well-being. Try keeping a journal, recording your thoughts and feelings as you 'step back'.

It isn't always easy. One woman told me that the only way she could find a little peace and space was to go into a cupboard in the attic in her house, well away from everyone.

Like most things worth doing, stepping back requires discipline. It needs to become a part of the routine of your life, and initially that means it will involve making an effort. But as with all good habits, when it has become a regular practice you will have discovered, as Confucius said, that 'silence is a true friend who never betrays'.

The great and the good who have relied on the regular practice of stepping back into a period of silence are many in number. As Blaise Pascal, the French mathematician and inventor, once said, 'All humanity's problems stem from man's inability to sit quietly in a room alone.'

When I was at Fitzwilliam College, Cambridge, studying law, I went on a silent retreat with some friends. As we sat over a lunch taken in complete silence we felt horribly uncomfortable and it was all we could do not to start giggling. What I wished for then, as did most of my friends, was to jump back into the car and return to college. But none of us wanted to be the first to give in, so we stuck it out – for the whole twenty-four hours. I am so glad we did, because the practice of silence has since had a remarkable impact on every stage of my life.

Henry David Thoreau, the American writer and passionate abolitionist, said that in order to preserve his health and spirits, he needed to spend at least four hours a day sauntering through the woods and over the hills, 'absolutely free from all worldly engagements'.

We haven't all got four hours to spend wandering, pleasant though that might be. So how, in today's world, do we begin to 'step back'?

There are essentially three ways: in small steps of no more than a few minutes, during everyday activities; in bigger steps of an hour or two, perhaps once or twice a week; or by taking a day or longer to go on retreat, either alone or with others.

Start Small

Small steps are the perfect way to start. Look for opportunities during your day to find a little peace and space. That means getting away from phones, computers and crowds. You can make space anywhere, but I find it works best when I can get out into natural surroundings. Go for a walk somewhere beautiful and peaceful, sit on a bench in the park, sit in your garden if you have one, but get outside – and fill your spirit with the peace and beauty of nature.

Don't mistake activity for stepping back. While an activity like cycling, surfing or running is good for you and can be cathartic, it's not the same as being peaceful and allowing space for reflection, the key factor in stepping back.

If you can't get outside, make space inside by

switching off the phone and relaxing somewhere comfortable and peaceful.

Here are a few suggestions of ways to 'step back' for five minutes during your day.

- Take a few minutes in the morning to reflect on how you'd like your day to be.
- While you are commuting, turn your phone off, sit quietly, close your eyes and turn your focus inwards. Reflect on your working day, and what you would like from it.
- Take a few minutes to listen to a beautiful piece of music.
- Find a café close to your home or work, choose a quiet corner and reflect over a coffee.
- Go to a library – they're wonderful places for peace and silence.
- Go for a peaceful, uninterrupted walk.
- Stop and sit on a bench.
- Look out of the window, focus on something natural, a tree or a patch of grass, and let your mind rest.
- Stop the car on the way home in a pleasant spot, get out and walk for a few minutes.
- Before you go to sleep, reflect on all the good things that have happened during the day.

Whenever you take a small 'step back', keep silent and allow your body to feel as relaxed as possible. Feel every muscle and sinew ease, release all the tension and then gradually empty your mind of all its clutter.

Once Buddha was walking with a few of his followers. While they were travelling, they happened to pass a lake. Buddha told one of his disciples, 'I am thirsty. Do get me some water from that lake there.'

The disciple walked up to the lake. When he reached it, he noticed that some people were washing clothes in the water and, right at that moment, a bullock cart started crossing through the lake. As a result, the water became very muddy. The disciple thought, 'How can I give this muddy water to Buddha to drink?'

So he came back and told Buddha, 'The water in there is very muddy. I don't think it is fit to drink.'

After about half an hour, Buddha asked the same disciple to go back to the lake and get him some water to drink. The disciple obediently went back to the lake. This time he found that the lake had absolutely clear water in it. The mud had settled. So he collected some water in a pot and brought it to Buddha.

Buddha said, 'See what you did to make the water clean. You let it be and the mud settled down on its own. Your mind is also like that. When it is disturbed, just let it be. Give it a little time. It will settle down on its own. You don't have to put in any effort to calm it down. It will happen.'

3

Alone

An hour or two once a week spent quietly alone in peaceful surroundings is of enormous value, and one day a month even more so.

Plan on being alone and in silence and, if you possibly can, get out into nature. In our fast, noisy world, moments of peace are rare, but the human spirit needs them. If you live with constant noise and distraction there is no space for a connection to your true self, to recharge your energy and to know your own thoughts and feelings.

If you can, take in the beauty of the landscape or the sea, listen to the rhythm of the life that thrives all around us, the lapping of the waves, the whispered resonances of the wind, the warmth and the light of the sun's rays or the sound of the rain falling on the leaves of trees.

Gradually in this way you will become aware of the sound of silence, of your mind slowing down and your heart becoming calm as you begin to breathe deeply and more regularly.

As you plan towards a period of stepping back in silence, large or small, you may find all sorts of competing claims racing around in your mind, all kinds of excuses as to how you could better spend your time. Just let these thoughts pass and head towards the silence anyway.

Allow your mind to be filled with good thoughts, banish negativity and remember those whom you love and who love you. Give thanks for them and for all the good things and people in your life, and begin to look for guidance towards the next steps of whatever challenges you face.

Some simple questions you can ask yourself:

- What is getting in the way?
- How responsible am I for that?
- What should I do next?

- What do I want to do more of?
- What am I not doing?
- What do I need to do next?

- What (or who) am I neglecting?
- What (or who) have I forgotten?
- What do I need to do?

- What is the most important thing I need to change in my life?
- What do I need to do to change it?
- What is possible, today?

By no means ask these questions all at once, but selectively, according to your circumstances or need or what's on your mind. Select one and discover where it leads you.

I've always been a passionate believer in making room in my life for peace and stillness: it is vitally important to me. I pack a lot in, but also make sure that I plan time for space. That's how I keep a balance in my life.

I make sure that, as well as a daily period of prayer and reflection each morning, I regularly put days in my diary when I am 'away' and not available for work. Then I take myself somewhere beautiful and spend time stepping back from the day-to-day bustle of life, to remind myself of what truly matters: my family, my health, my core purpose. For me that core purpose is about contribution and service, helping others to realise their potential.

Ramsay MacDonald, born the illegitimate son of a housemaid and a farm labourer, rose to be the first Labour prime minister of Britain in 1924 and a second time, as head of the National Government from 1931 to 1935. He grew up in farming communities in north-east Scotland and in later life he always talked about the Hill Road, the drovers' road close to his home where he loved to return to walk, and the vital role it played in giving him time and space for peace and reflection.

Taking a leaf from MacDonald's book, I call my time out – the periods of quietness and reflection – 'taking the Hill Road'. The Hill Road is where you go to be with yourself, to reflect, to know your own heart and discover or reignite your purpose. When people fail you, the Hill Road never does. Ramsay MacDonald said that it was on the Hill Road that he got his best wisdom and made his wisest decisions.

Sometimes one must flee from familiar things and faces and voices, from the daily round and the common task, because one's mind becomes a bit of green grass too much trod upon. It has to be protected and nursed, and it has to be let alone. Then, give me the hill road, the bleating of the sheep, the clouds, the sun and the rain, the graves of dead races, the thatched roofs of living ones, a pipe and a fire when the day is closing, and a clean bed to lie upon until the sun calls in the morning. If friends fail, the hill road never does.

Experiment with finding your own Hill Road. It might be your garden, a park or nearby open space. It doesn't have to be outside, but there is a healing energy in nature that can be very special.

For me, the place that fills my soul, replenishes me and allows me the deepest and most fundamental reflection is the Isle of Skye off the north-west coast of Scotland, a simply beautiful part of the world.

I knew Skye as a little boy only through the 'Skye Boat Song' that my mother used to sing to us. The song recalled the escape to Skye of Bonnie Prince Charlie after his defeat at the Battle of Culloden in 1746, but as I grew up I came to love the tune and the line 'Over the sea to Skye'. Even then it sounded far away and somehow special.

On Skye, walking over the hills, I have always found a sense of joy, calm and reconnection with myself. It is the place where I have regularly been able to take stock and to recharge.

The ACE Test

Here is a useful little test to apply when reviewing your life. It is simple but will tell you a great deal.

Ask yourself how much of you is given to each of the following in your life:

- Achievement
- Contribution
- Enjoyment

If you give yourself equally to all three, then your life is in balance. But if one is lacking, or the contribution is uneven, then recognising this will help you begin to redress the balance.

In 1997, as I stood on a hillside not far from our home on Skye, beside what my family call the Thinking Stone, I felt certain this was the place for the centre I had dreamed of building: a place where miracles of discovery and connection between people could happen and where young people from tough backgrounds could find belief in themselves and hope for their futures. There, where I had so often delighted in stepping back from my busy life, others might find the joy of stepping back – perhaps for the first time.

Of course, it isn't always possible to find somewhere beautiful and peaceful to just be, but there can still be ways to create the space to 'step back'. Ramsay MacDonald travelled by train from London to Scotland, consciously making the journey part of his transition to walk the Hill Road. I have done this myself. Some time ago I was due to travel from Edinburgh to London, and I was going with a heavy heart, having had to deal with a deeply distressing situation and being faced with a difficult decision. I knew that I needed to 'step back' for a period of personal reflection and reassessment before making that decision. I couldn't take time away, as I might have wished to do. Instead I chose to go by overnight train to London, rather than flying, in order to use that opportunity to 'step back' and reflect in the relative calm and quiet of an overnight journey.

4

With Others

While I feel we all need to 'step back' alone, it can also be of enormous benefit to 'step back' with a trusted other, such as a friend or colleague. Nothing is more important than human relationships, and the ability to create understanding, warmth and shared meaning with another person. This might be for deeper understanding, mutual support or to resolve a difficulty. Or it might be that one of you accompanies the other at a time of need.

I believe that *real, lasting change happens one on one, one by one, and then in partnership*. When we connect with one other person in a shared ideal, something magical begins to happen and together we can take the first step towards change.

Stepping back with another person provides an

opportunity for real communication. The power of effective communication can be summed up in one word: *depth*. We all communicate with others every day, exchanging greetings, information and news. But how often do we communicate with another person in depth? How often do we go deep inside to where the essence of a person lies, to discover their most hidden truths, feelings and hopes? It's no good just scratching the surface – that may make the world go round, but it doesn't actually help with anything significant. If we ask people to dig deep inside and if they trust us and feel comfortable, then things tumble out. And the experience can be incredibly cathartic.

I often coach people who lead incredibly busy lives and who say to me that they've never felt so alone, despite being surrounded by people all the time. It's because they are not really connecting with anyone. And the most powerful way to connect with another person is to listen to them, and have them listen to you.

When I am coaching people I probably speak for only 15 to 20 per cent of the time. The rest of the time, I listen and, in the space that listening creates, they feel able to open up and the potential for deeper connection is created.

It is important that the listening is genuine. If you listen to someone else with half an ear while actually thinking about other things, then you're not truly listening, and it will be a disappointing experience for both of you. Active listening involves engaging with what the other person is saying, taking it in and truly hearing their words and the feeling behind the words.

We all have a powerful need to be heard, without interruption or condemnation. There is a postbox hidden among the sand dunes on Bird Island, North Carolina. The box is marked 'Kindred Spirits', and inside are notebooks and pencils visitors can use to record their thoughts and prayers in complete anonymity. In the box people have written heartbreaking and moving confessions, secrets and prayers that they may never have shared with anyone else. To write their thoughts and feelings down and place them in a postbox on a secluded island is an indication of how much we long to be heard and witnessed. But if we can share that deep self-analysis with others, we have so much more chance of being helped and of helping others.

To share this kind of listening with another person while stepping back can be enormously rewarding. If we can hear one another, without judgement or justification, then we can create a deep and valuable connection between us.

5

Together With A Loved One

The best relationships are often sustained by regular periods of stepping back together, whether that is over a quietly shared meal, on a walk or in companionable silence in the car. Stepping back with a loved one can be a way of nurturing a relationship. A regular practice together becomes an appreciative one, and even with busy lives it is possible to integrate a daily period of stepping back.

My wife Elizabeth and I spend a few quiet minutes together each morning in prayer, and this small but very precious ritual prepares us for the day ahead.

However, it is when difficulties loom that stepping back can be at its most powerful and healing. An unexpected crisis such as worry about a child or loved one, dissatisfaction with or loss of a job or imminent redundancy or the threat of a serious illness can sow all sorts of seeds of anxiety and difficulty in any relationship. It is then that the practice of stepping back as a couple can help you to share and review your thinking and to talk about how matters might be addressed and what part each might play in partnership with the other. In this way many potential crises can be addressed before they are allowed to spiral out of control.

For a marriage or partnership that is in trouble, stepping back together can bring you closer in a way that seems miraculous. It provides a chance to rediscover one another, to review what has gone wrong, and to move forward.

When there is friction it can be a huge challenge to agree to 'step back' together and to commit to a time and place. But even if one or both of you are reluctant, it is worth the effort. Find as much goodwill as you can and allow time for each of you to listen to the other.

Stepping back with a loved one in this way can be a means of reminding ourselves of the best in one another, of the love you both feel and of your shared journey thus far. It can also provide a way to make fresh discoveries about one another, to express difficult feelings, and to rediscover the love which first brought you together.

On many occasions I have acted as an intermediary for couples stepping back for a day or more to review their relationship when it is in trouble or in need of renewed commitment. In a beautiful setting, away from everyday cares, with good food, a warm fire and the chance to walk and talk, many couples are able to turn a tense situation around and recommit to one another.

No matter the obstacles and difficulties and disappointments, great things can be achieved when good people come together in sincerity and in the quietness of their own hearts to look for a new way of doing things and a shared sense of purpose and happiness.

The CAN DO Test

This can be a great way of finding out where you are now, and where you want to go. Try it in a group setting, with a trusted other or on your own.

Challenges

Write them down, get them off your chest. What's wrong in your life? What haven't you said or done? Where do you need to let go?

Assets

Don't forget the diamonds you possess – the joy of family life, your values, trusted friends and colleagues, your own resilience and loyalty.

Non-negotiables

What are your red lines? What are you not prepared to give in over or trade, with yourself and with others? What are your essential principles and standards?

Direction(s)

Put the above – your Challenges, Assets and Non-negotiables – together, and see what Direction emerges. What needs to happen? What do you need to do?

Ownership

Own your choice of Direction, make it yours and get going on it. Plan out what you are going to do, in the short and the long term.

6

On Retreat

A retreat is a wonderful way of stepping back, and something I recommend everyone does once or twice a year. It might be an organised retreat, or one that you devise yourself. It can be with others, or alone. It should involve spending at least twenty-four hours, ideally longer – two or three days staying overnight in one place is a good length – away from home, in peaceful surroundings, and beautiful too if you can manage that, without computers, mobiles or any of the demands of your everyday life.

As someone who regularly conducts retreats, I have seen the enormous difference that being on retreat can make to even the most sceptical of participants. It doesn't seem like a very twenty-first-century thing to do – and it isn't. But that is precisely why it is so necessary and can be so special. Stepping back in this way is an immensely valuable investment in yourself, so it is worth making it a regular practice.

People tend to come to retreats exhausted and burned out. They arrive looking like rabbits caught in the headlights, worrying about what they should be doing back at the office. So I always make sure the first few hours of a retreat are about acclimatising – slowing down, mentally and physically. I give people time to let go of their busy 'work' personas and be themselves, to absorb the concept of time and have space simply to be.

Over the course of the retreat I see people change, as something begins to break through. Tired, tense people begin to lighten, to smile, to look around with new eyes. Enthusiasm returns, energy is restored, they are able to consider new ideas in a way that they previously felt too frantic and overwrought to do.

I believe that a day on retreat is worth at least two days of anything else. It isn't time lost from work, as it might seem: it's time gained, because you'll return to work reinvigorated.

Even a holiday is not the same as a retreat. Yes, holidays – at least when they go according to plan – can be relaxing and they provide a change of scene. Every now and then, a holiday might indeed be life-changing as you come to a big decision. But they do not consistently provide the depth and personal insight of a retreat.

People who retreat together bond in a different way. Whether they are partners in life, friends or work colleagues, they learn things about one another that they hadn't known, they get to know and understand one another better, and they reinforce shared ideals, ideas and hopes.

It's a joy to lead a retreat and it's always as much of a learning curve for me as it is for those taking part. Afterwards, participants regularly report real changes in the way that they operate, both individually and – if it's a work group – together within their organisation.

I am sometimes asked what the difference is between a leadership retreat and a training course. The answer, once again, is *depth*. A training course is great for teaching participants new information, ideas or skills, but it is programmed – the end is known from the beginning. A retreat is in some ways its opposite: nothing is predetermined, but in place of carefully prepared lessons a retreat will ask those participating to look deep inside themselves for the truths, dreams and hopes that they seldom consider or reveal. The benefits are so much greater as a result.

A successful executive on one of our retreats might find themselves asking, 'Who might I have been – what else might I have done?' They may wonder why they took endless exams but never identified what they really wanted in life. A young person attending a Columban Leadership Academy (which is another tried and tested way of stepping back) might discover, 'I do have something to give after all, I am someone worthwhile, I have things I want to do and achieve.'

When I am conducting leadership retreats, around Britain and in various parts of the world, I often refer to the Hand of Mandela. This is an ink handprint of Nelson Mandela's right hand. Mandela was a keen artist and this print was said to have been created by accident while he was working on a sketch inspired by his 27-year imprisonment, nine of them in solitary confinement, on Robben Island. What is extraordinary about the handprint is that in the palm there is a perfect outline of the African continent. It is almost as if the land he loved so much is imprinted in his hand, and in his soul.

Nelson Mandela was a man whose courage, compassion and humanity helped him to lead South Africa to freedom, and made him a beacon of hope to oppressed people throughout the world. He always reached out his hands to others, to connect, to bring them together and to offer friendship, so I like to use the handprint as a symbol of connection between retreat participants. I suggest that they use it as the basis of a take-home message; the palm of the hand is the essence of all they have discovered and each of the fingers and the thumb represents something they will do, or change. For instance, they might intend to spend more time with their children, take more regular exercise, be more loving towards a partner, delegate more and put aside regular time for reflection.

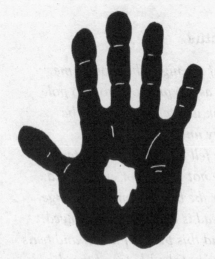

One of the poems I often share is 'Invictus', by the Victorian poet William Ernest Henley. The title was later used for a 2009 film, telling the story of how Nelson Mandela, then South African president, joined forces with Francois Pienaar, captain of the Springboks, to inspire the South African rugby team to win the 1995 Rugby World Cup. The tournament was held in South Africa following the dismantling of apartheid, and winning it sent a hugely powerful message about freedom, courage and the need to build the Rainbow Nation.

'Invictus', a word which can be translated from the Latin as 'undefeated', or 'unconquered', was written by Henley when he was still only a teenager, after his leg was amputated as a result of tuberculosis. It is a testament to overcoming pain and difficulty, and Nelson Mandela often quoted from it as a source of inspiration and strength.

Invictus

Out of the night that covers me
Black as the pit from pole to pole
I thank whatever gods may be
For my unconquerable soul.
In the fell clutch of circumstance
I have not winced or cried aloud.
Under the bludgeoning of change
My head is bloody, but unbowed.
Beyond this place of wrath and tears
Looms but the horror of the shade
And yet the menace of the years
Find and shall find me unafraid.
It matters not how strait the gate
How charged with punishment the scroll.
I am the Master of my fate
I am the Captain of my soul.

I encourage everyone who comes on a retreat to engage with this poem: I want them to feel that they can be *the captain of their soul* and *the master of their fate*.

Too many people feel buffeted by the decisions of others. A recent survey found that no less than half the people working in the public sector feel that they are not in control of their working lives, and are bored and frustrated. A retreat is an opportunity to take a fresh look at what you are doing and to decide whether – and how – you want to go on. It is always valuable to remind yourself why you are doing what you do.

We live in an age when, due to constraints of time and the pressure to achieve measurable results, many occupations have become mechanised and soulless. Medicine is a prime example. Traditionally one of the caring professions, now GPs have ten minutes in which to see each patient. In that time it is often impossible to get to the bottom of what might well be a complex problem. All too often the patient leaves feeling unheard and anxious, while the doctor feels dissatisfied because they have not been able to give of their best. To 'step back' is an opportunity for the doctor to remember why they chose medicine, and what really matters in what they do.

A doctor who attended a two-day retreat wrote:

I had almost lost sight of why I came into medicine in the first place, but now there is a spring in my step, having had the chance to work with my colleagues and learn more about myself. I have been challenged and encouraged and shown my inner strength and this has given me time to take stock about what I am trying to do within the profession I love. Above all else, I have been inspired to be even better and for that I am most humbly grateful.

A head teacher in a 'tough reality' area with plenty of problems already on her desk was facing the prospect of an enforced merger of two schools, and she had been appointed the new head of the joint school. She took the opportunity to 'step back' in a leadership retreat, where she was able to discuss the new challenge with other head teachers and representatives from the educational directorate:

It reminded me of the strength of talent and the array of skills and support that exist. I know I will continue to evolve and change as a result of this experience. I cannot help feeling that there is already a noticeable change in how we are all working together in the best interests of the young people for whom we have responsibility in our schools and not least in our new school merger project.

What a gift it is to be freshly inspired about what you do. Too often people feel weighed down by red tape, bureaucracy and paperwork, to the point that it becomes easy to lose sight of the profession you chose and loved. To cut through all the layers and get back to the heart of what you do, reconnecting with your reasons for doing it in the first place, is like digging through layer upon layer of dark, black mud and finding a diamond.

This is the gift of stepping back on a retreat. It allows you to establish enough distance from everyday life, and enough time, to rediscover your true purpose or perhaps to discover your real purpose in life for the first time.